BEYOND THE TREELINE

BY RYAN THOMPSON

INTRODUCTION

GROWING UP, MY DAD always had a Gifford Pinchot National Forest map laid out on the kitchen table. Its creases and folds showed all the adventures we had together. This map was more than just paper; it was our ticket to exploring nature and discovering its beauty. The forest, home to the famous Mount St. Helens, became our playground, a vast area waiting for us to uncover its secrets. We explored every inch we could find, from the calm waters of Packwood Lake, where the tall trees reflected on the surface, to the steep trails of Badger Peak that challenged us, and the peaceful shores of Coldwater Lake. Each trail we hiked added a new memory to our adventure, showing our love for the wilderness.

As a kid, I started highlighting on Dad's Gifford Pinchot map to record our travels. I highlighted the trails and roads we took, remembering the unique things we saw and the wildlife we encountered. I made it a goal to explore the more than one million acres of this national forest, dreaming of the day I could say I had seen it all. It was a big dream, but it filled me with excitement and purpose, fueling my adventurous spirit and love for nature. Each hike was not just an adventure, but also a chance to connect with my Dad and the amazing landscapes around us, creating lasting memories in the heart of nature.

In 2006, my life took an unexpected turn when I received a diagnosis of Multiple Sclerosis (MS). This news hit me hard after I had been experiencing troubling symptoms while hiking with my Dad. I remember feeling scared and overwhelmed, and I could have easily let this diagnosis shatter my spirit. Instead, it sparked a fire within me that I didn't know was there. I adopted a new mantra: to push through no matter what challenges came my way. I found strength in the verse from Nehemiah 8:10, which says, "The joy of the Lord is your strength." This became my anchor during what felt like the toughest times in my recovery journey.

Multiple Sclerosis (MS) is a chronic disease that affects the central nervous system, which comprises the brain and spinal cord. It occurs when the immune system mistakenly attacks the protective covering of nerve fibers, known as myelin, leading to communication problems between the brain and the rest of the body. This disruption can result in a variety of symptoms, including fatigue, difficulty walking, numbness, and vision problems. The severity and progression of MS can vary widely from person to person, with some individuals experiencing mild symptoms and others facing significant challenges in their daily lives. Despite the overwhelming nature of this diagnosis, many people with MS find ways to adapt, seek treatment, and continue pursuing their passions, demonstrating remarkable resilience and strength.

The early days following my diagnosis were incredibly challenging and filled with uncertainty. I found myself struggling with basic tasks, like walking, and there were moments when I completely lost my mobility. Each setback was frustrating and sometimes disheartening, but I was determined not to let MS define who I was or how I lived my life. I knew I had to find a way to adapt and keep moving forward, no matter how tough things got. That's when I discovered cycling.

Cycling became my outlet. By clipping my feet into the pedals, I was able to regain some control and independence, even with my limited mobility. The sensation of propelling myself forward on the bike gave me a sense of freedom that I desperately needed. I pushed myself harder than ever, determined to overcome the obstacles MS placed in my path. Each time I got on the bike, I felt a little more like myself again.

It was during this transformative phase that I set my sights on a new goal: the Loowit Trail. The term "Loowit" originated from the language of the local Klickitat tribe, reflecting their deep-rooted connection to the land. For the native people, the mountain held cultural and spiritual significance, revered not only for its majestic beauty but also as a symbol of resilience and transformation through its volcanic activity. By choosing to pursue the Loowit Trail, I aimed to honor this rich heritage while forging my own path of strength and perseverance in the face of Multiple Sclerosis. This trail is a challenging and ever-shifting path that encircles Mount St. Helens. I was captivated by its beauty and the thrill of tackling something so daunting. The thought of hiking this incredible trail filled me with excitement and anticipation. I knew it would take a lot of hard work and perseverance to prepare for this adventure, but I was ready to embrace the challenge.

I started training rigorously with cycling, gradually building my strength and endurance. The journey ahead would not only test my physical limits but also strengthen my resolve and spirit as I continued to navigate life with MS. Each day on the bike was a step closer to my goal, and I began to feel a deep sense of accomplishment.

As I trained, I also connected with others in the cycling community who inspired me with their own stories of overcoming challenges. Their support and encouragement fueled my motivation even more. I learned that I wasn't alone in my struggles, and that made a significant difference in my journey.

Preparing for the Loowit Trail became more than just a physical challenge; it was a way for me to reclaim my life and prove to myself that I could achieve great things despite my condition. The experience taught me valuable lessons about resilience, determination, and the importance of setting goals. I was excited to see what I could accomplish as I continued forward, embracing the ups and downs along the way.

The Loowit Trail presented the perfect challenge for any outdoor enthusiast. Its length varied with each season, stretching anywhere from 30 to nearly 40 miles, depending on the conditions of its pumice-filled base. This meant that every season one attempted the trail, they faced a new adventure, as the terrain could change dramatically with the weather and time of year. To add to the excitement, there was no direct access to the trail itself; it could only be reached through a series of feeder trails. This unpredictability and the challenging nature of the route made it a true test of my endurance and willpower.

This book is a collection of snippets from my journey to conquer the Loowit Trail. I discovered that tackling this extreme trail required me to break it down into smaller, manageable sections. By embracing each part of the trek, I was able to fully appreciate the beauty and challenges it offered. Each hike along the Loowit Trail was unique, filled with breathtaking sights such as stunning views of nearby mountains, lush forests, and vibrant wildflowers, alongside unforgettable memories that I will cherish forever.

Throughout this experience, my determination to not let a disability stand in my way became a powerful driving force that fueled my perseverance. Each step I took along the trail was a testament to my strength and resilience. I learned that the journey was not just about reaching the end but about enjoying the incredible adventures along the way. The Loowit Trail taught me valuable lessons about overcoming obstacles, embracing challenges, and finding joy in the journey itself.

Throughout the years, my health has gone through many ups and downs, but I always faced each challenge head-on. With every effort I made, my body responded in different ways. Sometimes it pushed back, reminding me of its limits, but more often than not, it amazed me with its strength and resilience. This book tells the story of those experiences, capturing my journey of rising above obstacles and thriving even when the odds seemed stacked against me. It serves as a tribute to the incredible power of determination, showcasing how one's will can overcome difficulties. It also highlights the beauty found in nature and the strong, unbreakable bond that exists between my Heavenly Father and His child. As I navigated through tough times, my relationship with the Lord deepened, proving that love and support can be a guiding light in dark moments. Through these pages, I hope to inspire others to embrace their own journeys, no matter how challenging they may be.

LOOWIT FALLS

THE DRIVE ALONG HIGHWAY 504 was always a prelude to the adventure that awaited us. This curvy ribbon of asphalt, officially known as Washington State Route 504, wound its way through the lush forests and up the rugged terrain towards Mount St. Helens. Each twist and turn felt like it was teasing us with glimpses of what lay ahead—an epic journey around the iconic volcano. The road itself seemed to breathe with life, bordered by towering evergreens and occasionally opening up to reveal breathtaking vistas of the Toutle River valley below.

As Dad and I wound our way up the highway, I couldn't help but reflect on our countless conversations about this trip. The Loowit Trail had been a multi-year dream of mine, a symbol of perseverance and pushing limits, especially for someone like me battling Multiple Sclerosis. Diagnosed the year I graduated high school, I had faced the disease head-on and embraced the challenge. My mom was diagnosed with MS when I was just three months old, so you could say I was quite familiar with the prognosis. Two things I had learned from my family were to never give up and to savor the view along the way.

The Loowit Trail is no ordinary hike. Encircling Mount St. Helens, it spans over thirty to forty miles and weaves through diverse landscapes shaped by the mountain's dramatic 1980 eruption. With no direct trailhead parking, access to Loowit requires navigating secondary or "feeder" trails. From towering lava formations and barren pumice plains to verdant forests regaining life, the trail offers both breathtaking beauty and challenging terrain. For many, it's a test of endurance and spirit, demanding resilience and determination at every turn.

The anticipation was palpable as we drove higher, the air growing thinner, cooler, and filled with the scent of pine and earth, which seemed to carry whispers of ancient stories waiting to be discovered. The sound of our car engine humming along the path was peaceful, blending seamlessly with the occasional calls of birds, the rustling of leaves, and the distant gurgle of a hidden stream.

We finally reached the Johnston Ridge Observatory parking lot, the starting point of our trek. Getting out of the car, we were greeted by other hikers preparing for their own adventures. Their faces were a mix of excitement and determination, some chiseling away at last minute preparations while others stood quietly, soaking in the majestic view. The observatory itself stood proudly, offering panoramic views of the volcano and its surrounding landscape, a reminder of nature's incredible power and beauty. Its walls were adorned with informative plaques and photographs that depicted the catastrophic eruption of 1980, a stark contrast to the serene beauty of wild flowers and returning trees that now surrounded us.

Dad began unpacking the supplies, an assortment of trail mix, chocolate, and water—a testament to his adventure mindset. He double checked our gear, ensuring we had everything we needed for the challenging trek ahead. The sun was beginning to cast long shadows, signaling the late morning start, and a cool breeze carried with it the promise of a peaceful evening. The sky was a brilliant blue, with only a few wispy clouds drifting lazily by, and the distant peaks seemed to glow with a soft, golden light.

As we geared up, I noticed Dad's calm demeanor, the kind that balanced out my growing anxiety. His methodical way of checking and rechecking our gear was both comforting and inspiring, a quiet assurance that we were prepared for the journey ahead. The weight of my backpack felt substantial, but it was a burden I was ready to bear, a physical manifestation of the inner strength I had cultivated over the past year of managing my condition. Each item in my pack had been carefully chosen, from the sturdy hiking boots to the custom wood trekking poles that my Dad spent countless hours crafting for us both, all essentials for our survival and comfort on the trail.

"Ready, Ryan?" Dad asked, his eyes filled with a quiet determination that mirrored my own hopes and fears.

"Ready as I'll ever be," I replied, tightening the straps on my backpack and taking a deep breath of the crisp, clean air. The path before us was challenging, but it was a challenge we were ready to face together. As we took our first steps onto the trail, I felt a surge of exhilaration, knowing that this journey would test our limits and forge unforgettable memories.

The trail stretched out before us, winding through the wilderness, promising both trials and triumphs along the way. The first section led us through a regrowing forest, where the smell of damp earth and the sound of rustling leaves enveloped us in nature's embrace. Although the mountain erupted in 1980, the forest has been slow to recover. It still has a long way to go before becoming a mighty forest once more. We traversed ash, pumice, and rocks, each step a vivid reminder of the rugged terrain awaiting us. Occasionally, we would come across small patches of wildflowers that dotted the desolate and regrowing floor with splashes of color.

As we continued, the trail gave way to a landscape marked by the raw power of the volcanic eruption. The trees gradually became sparser. The ground was covered in ash and pumice, a stark contrast to the verdant forest that covered the rest of Western Washington. Yet, even in this seemingly barren wasteland, life found a way. Hardy shrubs and tenacious wildflowers clung to the rocky soil, their resilience a testament to nature's indomitable spirit.

Lupines, with their jasmine-like fragrance, have always been my favorite wildflowers. On the other hand, Indian Paintbrushes, in their rare and vibrant shades of orange and red, were my Dad's favorite. It was incredible to witness the abundance of these wildflowers everywhere we looked.

We paused frequently to take in the view, each stop offering a new perspective on the majestic Mount St. Helens. The mountain loomed large in the distance, its snow-capped rim glistening in the morning sunlight. The sight was both awe-inspiring and humbling, a reminder of the forces that shape our world. With each step, we drew closer to our goal, driven by a shared sense of purpose and the promise of the adventure that lay ahead.

The first steps onto the Truman Trail were both exhilarating and daunting. Named after Harry R. Truman, the stubborn old man who famously refused to leave his lodge during the catastrophic eruption of Mount St. Helens in 1980, the trail itself was a mix of awe-inspiring beauty and treacherous paths carved by nature's fury. Small, Christmas-sized trees framed the path, their needles waving in the wind. The distant sound of rushing water hinted at an unseen stream meandering through the hillside. The air was crisp and the sky overhead was a brilliant blue, dotted with the occasional fluffy cloud.

We moved cautiously along the cliff sides, where one misstep could spell disaster and send us plummeting into the abyss below. My foot drop was an unwelcome companion today, making each step feel like lifting a lead weight. My legs, already betraying me, started to feel like jello, wobbling with every movement. Anxiety crept in, a relentless shadow that threatened to paralyze my progress with each uncertain step. The trail's uneven terrain, with its loose rocks, sudden drops, and sand-like pumice, didn't make it any easier. Each obstacle seemed to mock my every effort, challenging my resolve.

But Dad was there, as always on the trail, steady and unflinching, his presence a beacon of stability. "Just focus on one step at a time," he said, his voice a soothing anchor in the turbulent sea of my mind. "We'll get through this together." Every step was a battle, but with Dad's encouragement, I found the strength to push forward. He pointed out interesting flora along the way, like the hardy wildflowers that bravely sprouted from cracks in the rock, seemingly defying the odds. These small bursts of color amidst the barren trail provided momentary distractions from the strain of the hike.

As we carefully navigated this particularly tricky section of the trail, we noticed movement at the bottom of the steep mountainside. There, running away in the distance, was a majestic herd of elk. Even from afar, their sheer size was captivating, each one appearing massive against the landscape. They moved with a graceful yet powerful rhythm, their bodies blending seamlessly with the moss and ash. It was a fleeting but mesmerizing sight, one that momentarily lifted the weight of my struggles, reminding me of the breathtaking beauty and wildness of nature that lay just beyond my reach.

Dad's slow and steady pace was a constant reminder of his resilience, a trait I desperately tried to emulate. After taking a much needed break to observe the herd of elk, it was time to press on and match Dad's inspiring pace. The trail continued to wind through the landscape, each bend revealing new challenges and breathtaking vistas.

With Dad nearby, I felt a renewed determination to face whatever lay ahead. His knack for storytelling kept my mind occupied, as he recounted tales of his own adventures and the history of the area. Each story was a lesson in perseverance and wonder, reminding me that the journey, no matter how arduous, was part of what made the experience so rewarding.

Dad's stories soon turned to a time before the eruption of Mount St. Helens, when the area was a bustling hub for outdoor enthusiasts. In the decades leading up to the catastrophic 1980 eruption, Mount St. Helens had been a magnet for tourists eager to witness its towering presence and lush, surrounding wilderness. Visitors flocked to the area for its unrivaled camping, hiking, and fishing opportunities. The pristine Spirit Lake, nestled at the mountain's base, was a particularly popular destination, drawing tourists with its serene waters and scenic backdrop.

He went on to talk about how the local tourism industry thrived, with small businesses carving out their niches catering to the needs of the adventurers who descended upon the region. Cabins, lodges, and campsites dotted the landscape, while rental shops provided gear for those keen on exploring the mountain's trails or the lake's clear waters. Guided tours offered an even closer look at the mountain's grandeur, with knowledgeable locals sharing stories about the area's rich geological history.

In the towns nearby, festivals and events celebrating the natural beauty and the thriving community spirit were commonplace. These gatherings not only showcased the region's attractions but also bolstered the livelihoods of many who depended on tourism. The area's vibrant tourism scene served as a testament to the enduring allure of Mount St. Helens, long before its serene visage was forever altered by the eruption.

His stories always fascinated me. It was like having a personal tour guide at your beck and call, whether you wanted one or not. Some of the stories I had heard several times, but I always welcomed hearing them again.

Dad continued on to recount the time his group of friends decided to trek through the snow covered trails surrounding the mountain, eager to experience the it's beauty in a different season. Bundled up in their warmest gear, they set off with high spirits, navigating through the crisp, white landscape. The snow crunched beneath their boots as they made their way deeper into the wilderness.

However, as the daylight waned and the snowfall began to intensify, the trail markers became increasingly difficult to spot. Before long, they realized they were lost. Despite their best efforts to retrace their steps, the familiar paths had vanished under a fresh blanket of snow. Panic started to set in as temperatures dropped and visibility worsened.

Huddling together for warmth, they debated their next move, trying to stay calm amid the mounting fear.

Fortunately, Dad's keen sense of direction and the group's collective perseverance eventually led them to a recognizable landmark—a towering old growth tree they had passed earlier in the day. Using this as their guide, they managed to navigate back to the main trail and, with a renewed sense of determination, found their way back to the car. The relief they felt upon seeing the vehicle was immense, and the experience, despite its challenges, became one of the most memorable and cherished stories of their youth.

I always found myself getting lost in Dad's stories. They made the time fly by, almost as if the clock stopped itself. But another set of red Indian Paintbrushes caught his eye, momentarily pulling him away from his tales. He took out his camera and started clicking, capturing all the best shots he could.

As the day wore on and the sun began to become unbearably hot, we reached a particularly stunning viewpoint. From this vantage, we could see the sprawling landscape below, a patchwork of pumice covered plains, rivers, and valleys, all bathed in the sun's golden light. Mt. St. Helen's loomed overhead, it was a breathtaking moment. Click. Add another 50 pictures to the camera's storage. It was a moment of pure serenity, a reminder of why we had embarked on this journey in the first place.

Despite the physical and mental challenges, the Truman Trail was a testament to the beauty and resilience found in both nature and ourselves. And with each step, I was reminded that, with support and determination, even the most daunting paths can lead to the most rewarding destinations.

Leaving the cliff sides behind, we entered the Pumice Plains, a vast, desolate expanse that stretched as far as the eye could see. This almost entirely treeless terrain, blanketed in shifting pumice and ash, felt like stepping onto another planet. The ground was unstable, each step sinking slightly, making forward motion even more challenging. The air was filled with a fine, gritty dust that clung to our clothes and got into every crevice, irritating our skin and eyes. Yet, the surreal landscape was captivating, a stark reminder of the mountain's fiery past where a violent eruption had left a lasting scar on the earth.

The sun blazed down on us, its rays relentless and unforgiving, reflecting off the gray pumice and intensifying the heat. Sweat dripped down my face, and my skin began to burn despite the generous amount of sunscreen I had applied in the morning. The trifecta of wind, sun, and ash burn became a very real threat. My water bottle was quickly depleting, and the heat was sapping our energy with every passing minute. Still, the sight of Loowit Falls in the very far distance spurred us on. It was a glimmer of hope, a tangible goal that made each grueling step worth it. The falls shimmered like a mirage, beckoning us with the promise of cool, refreshing water.

As we trekked on, the path seemed to grow increasingly arduous. Our legs felt heavy, and the constant slipping in the loose pumice made progress slow. The landscape around us, though barren in the traditional sense, was filled with wildflowers and hardy plants that had somehow managed to take root in this inhospitable environment. These tiny bursts of color against the gray ash reminded us once again of nature's remarkable resilience.

After several hours of hiking, each one feeling more arduous than the last, we finally reached the falls. The sound of cascading water was a song of victory, a reward for our efforts that rejuvenated our spirits. The waterfall plunged from a high cliff directly out of the crater, creating a misty spray that cooled our overheated bodies. We stopped to take in the view, the falls a breathtaking spectacle against the barren landscape, a striking contrast of life and desolation. The water seemed icy cold, unfortunately we were unable to touch the water due to the ever shifting steep pumice banks it flowed through. This moment of respite allowed us to truly appreciate the rugged beauty of nature.

Loowit Falls is one of the most captivating features along the Loowit Trail. This waterfall cascades gracefully from a height of approximately 200 feet, originating from the meltwater of Mount St. Helens' glaciers. It pours straight out of the crater. The roaring sound of the falls can be heard from quite a distance.

Standing at the base of Mount St. Helens, you are greeted by the awe-inspiring sight of the crater glacier. Formed in the aftermath of the 1980 eruption, this glacier has steadily grown over the years, filling the horseshoe shaped crater with its icy expanse. The glacier is a dazzling blue-white, a stark contrast to the rugged, gray walls of the crater and growing dome that surround it.

As you gaze up, the sheer scale of the mountain and the glacier becomes evident. The cold, crisp air carries the faint scent of earth and rock, a reminder of the cataclysmic forces that once reshaped this landscape. The views from here are nothing short of epic. The glacier appears almost otherworldly, snaking its way around the crater, with crevasses that hint at its slow but powerful movement.

From this vantage point, the panorama is breathtaking. The jagged peaks of the crater rim rise sharply against the sky, while the glacier gleams below, a testament to nature's resilience and beauty. The sense of isolation and grandeur is palpable, making every step on the Loowit Trail feel like a journey into the heart of the wild. This moment, standing at the foot of the crater opening, embodies the spirit of adventure and the raw, untamed beauty of the Pacific Northwest.

We lingered by the falls for a while, savoring the cool air and the soothing sound of the water. It was a sanctuary amidst the harshness of the Pumice Plains, a place where we could recharge before continuing our journey. As we prepared to leave, we filled our water bottles nearby with the crisp, clear water from a small spring, knowing it would sustain us on our way back. This experience had not only tested our physical endurance but also deepened our respect for the untamed wilderness. The memory of Loowit Falls, shimmering like a beacon in the barren landscape, would stay with us long after we had returned to the comfort of our daily lives.

The simple act of eating and drinking water felt like the greatest luxury. I was on cloud 9 with my Dad. We sat on a few large boulders near the trail, the sun frying us from above, casting a harsh glow on our surroundings. Water filled, we decided to sit down and rest for a little bit more before we headed back to the car. The 8+ mile trek wasn't one meant to be rushed, our goal was to enjoy every moment we could. We talked about life, our dreams, and the challenges we faced, both big and small. It was in these moments that I felt a deep connection with him, his wisdom a guiding light through the complexities of my life.

"You know, Ryan," Dad said, looking out at the cascading falls, a majestic sight that seemed to hold a thousand secrets, "it's not just about reaching the destination. It's about the journey, the struggles, and how we overcome them."

His words resonated deeply with me, a reminder that my battle with MS was just part of my journey, not the definition of it. It was a profound moment, the sound of the falls creating a natural soundtrack that underscored his advice. I felt a renewed sense of resolve and clarity.

As we began the journey back, the path seemed a little less daunting. The desolate landscape around us, oddly felt like a protective embrace. Each step was still a struggle, my muscles protesting, but now it was imbued with a sense of accomplishment. We had conquered this section of the trail, together, and that was a victory in itself.

Step by step, we made our way back to the Johnston Ridge Observatory parking lot, the setting sun casting a golden hue over everything. We paused frequently, taking in the fresh mountain air and the panoramic views that stretched out before us once more. The interplay of light and shadow on the landscape created a breathtaking tableau, nature's artistry in full display. We were tired but fulfilled, ready to face whatever the next leg of our journey would bring.

The day had given us more than just memories; it had given us a deeper bond and a shared sense of triumph. As we reached the car, I looked back at the trail, feeling a sense of gratitude for the day's experiences. The challenges we had faced now seemed like stepping stones towards conquering this trail. The journey wasn't over, but had only just begun. This adventure was beginning to sink in with just how big it would be.

WINDY PASS

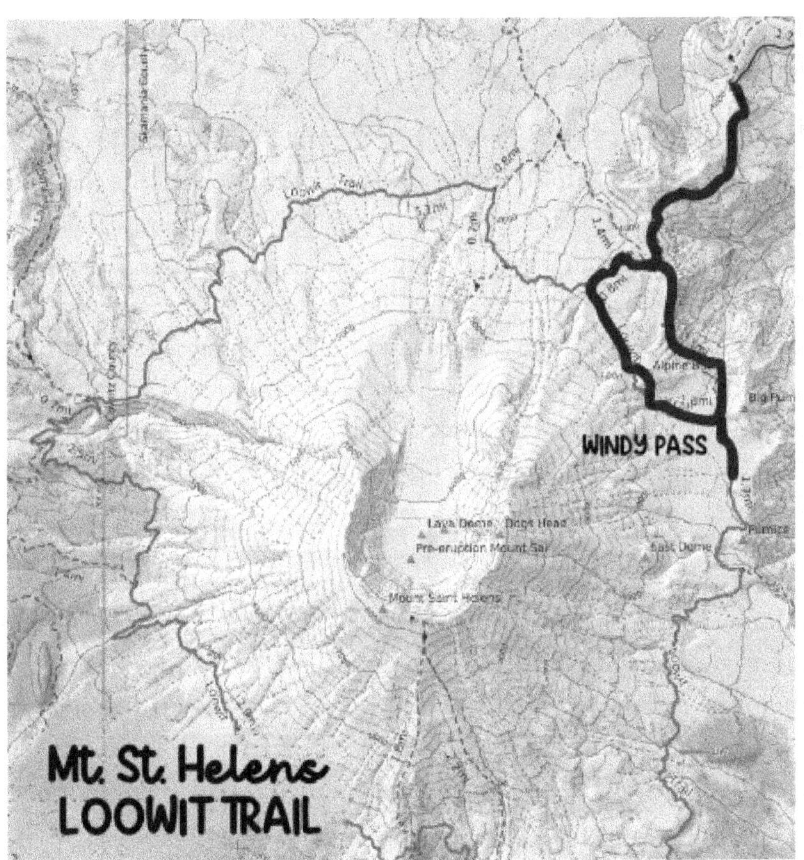

OUR JOURNEY BEGAN AT Forest Road 26, a hidden gem that sets the stage for the off-the-beaten-path adventures we cherish. The drive itself was an adventure, winding through dense forests and remote wilderness that whispered promises of the untamed beauty awaiting us. With my Dad behind the wheel and my brother navigating, we felt a mix of anticipation and excitement. We passed towering Douglas firs that seemed to touch the sky, and occasionally, the sunlight would break through the canopy, casting a magical glow on the road. The air was crisp and filled with the earthy scent of fallen leaves and pine needles. Along the way, we spotted deer grazing peacefully and heard the distant call of birds. Every twist and turn in the road brought us deeper into nature's embrace, making us feel both small and profoundly connected to the world around us.

Turning off Forest Road 25 onto Forest Road 99, we began to notice a shift in the landscape. The dense forest gradually opened up, revealing glimpses of the majestic mountain ahead. As we journeyed along the road, the trees thinned out, and expansive views of the rugged terrain unfolded before us. The air became cooler and fresher, invigorating our senses. Each bend in the road offered more stunning vistas, with the mountain's snow covered peaks growing ever more prominent against the sky. By the time we approached the Windy Ridge viewpoint, the mountain stood in full splendor, its grandeur a breathtaking reward for the start of today's hiking adventure.

The sun was already high, casting long shadows over the rugged volcanic landscape around us. Windy Ridge viewpoint stood spectacularly, with its staircase containing over a hundred steps rising above the parking lot, each step a testament to the effort required for such a remarkable vantage point. The steep steps challenged hikers but promised a reward at the summit. Reaching the top was no small feat, but the view that awaited kept spirits high. At the pinnacle, an awe inspiring panorama greeted hikers, offering a sweeping, unobstructed view of Mount St. Helens, its crater, and the vast surrounding landscape.

As a child, climbing the stairs up the mountain at Windy Ridge filled me with both excitement and a sense of accomplishment. Each visit began with an eager dash at the base of the stairs, my small legs pumping with enthusiasm. However, this burst of energy quickly waned as I faced the imposing large steps. It took two to three of my small steps to conquer just one of those giant steps. The stairs were uniquely structured, with the outside framed by sturdy wood and the interior filled with shifting, weightless pumice and ash. This uneven surface added an extra layer of challenge, making each ascent feel like a mini conquest. Despite the initial rush and the subsequent slow-down, the promise of the view from the top was a powerful motivator that kept me pushing forward, step by step, until I reached the summit.

Despite the memories of the stairs flooding back, the view from the parking lot or the hill above wasn't our focus today. Our objective was to complete a loop that would take us through several trails, leading to Windy Pass and the legendary Plains of Abraham on the northeast and eastern side of Mt. St. Helens. We gathered our gear, conducted last minute checks to ensure nothing was forgotten, and passed around the metal service access gate marking the start of our journey on the south side of the parking lot.

With excitement and anticipation, we embarked on our trek towards Windy Pass, eager to explore the natural beauty and stunning vistas that lay ahead. The trail, renowned for its breathtaking viewpoints and resilient fauna, promised an adventure filled with wonder and reflection. As we hiked, the crisp mountain air filled with hints of wind spun ash inflated our lungs, invigorating our spirits and heightening our appreciation for the surrounding beauty.

The initial stretch of Trail #216E presented a gentle climb, leading us upwards through a stunning array of wildflowers. During the blooming season, the trail is adorned with vibrant lupines and Indian paintbrushes, their vivid colors standing in stark contrast to the desolate volcanic terrain around us. The rich hues and fragrant scents were a sensory delight, transforming the early ascent into a truly delightful experience. We stopped frequently to admire the flora and fauna, capturing photos of the picturesque landscape as we made our way towards a rocky promontory overlooking Windy Pass.

As we pressed on, the trail guided us westward, ascending steadily towards our goal: the Loowit Trail #216. Upon arriving at the junction, we turned left and continued uphill toward Windy Pass.

The path became more challenging as we approached the pass, with steep and narrow switchbacks testing our endurance and pushing our physical limits. Each step required careful navigation, and the higher we climbed, the more relentless the ascent became.

Despite our determination, my legs began to grow weak from uncontrollable muscle spasms, a disheartening effect of my Multiple Sclerosis. Each step felt increasingly arduous, as if a heavy weight was tethering me to the rugged earth. My muscles quivered uncontrollably, making it difficult to maintain my balance on the narrow switchbacks. The harsh realization of my physical limitations loomed large.

A barrage of discouraging thoughts clouded my mind, whispering that I should turn back, that I wasn't strong enough to continue. But amidst the doubt, a quiet but resolute Holy Spirit surfaced, reminding me why I embarked on this trek in the first place. It urged me to focus on the resilient spirit within me, the one that refuses to yield to adversity. Drawing strength from the stunning vistas and the unwavering support of my family, I took a deep breath and pressed on, each step a testament to my resolve and my refusal to let Multiple Sclerosis dictate my life's adventures.

Step by step, we breached the pass. The sun was beating down intensely, and combined with the wind, it created a deadly duo. My brother and I posed for a few quick photos, laughing as we checked off this milestone from our list. Ironically, I would revisit this pass several more times in the future, each occasion no less challenging than the first. Windy was a difficult, shifting pass, and each successful hike was an achievement worth celebrating.

Navigating the backside of Windy Pass proved tricky. The ever shifting pumice made the trail difficult to discern, causing our family to scatter as we tried to find our way. We lost sight of the trail multiple times, each instance more disorienting than the last. Sliding down the treeless pumice-filled hillside with no trail in sight became an all too frequent occurrence.

The heat and pass began to take its toll on me, exacerbating my health even more. My legs were losing their strength yet again, each step becoming more laborious as I struggled to maintain my balance on the shifting pumice. Despite the challenges, my brother remained steadfast by my side, ensuring I was okay. "Just a little further," he would say, his voice a mixture of encouragement and concern. In my mind, I questioned whether I'd be able to continue. I didn't believe my brother's encouragement and started to believe the lie that this would never end.

The relentless sun paired with the unstable ground felt overwhelming, but the determination in my brother's eyes gave me the resolve to push forward. Each time I faltered, he was there, a constant reminder that we were in this together. The thought of letting him down fueled my perseverance, even as every muscle in my body screamed for respite.

The realization that there was no water available hit us hard when we reached a huge completely dry river bed at the start of the Plains of Abraham. Signs of heat stroke began to show among us in the relentless heat, wind, and ash burn. There was not much we could do except to continue trekking along. The views to the south and southeast inspired us to keep moving. It included glimpses of Mount Hood, adding to the dramatic moon like scenery. The trail crossed just a short distance of the flat Plains of Abraham before reaching Trail #216D, where we turned left to head back towards the trailhead.

Piles of stones served as markers for the trail on the treeless pumice plain, guiding our steps through the desolate yet mesmerizing expanse. History notes that this area, even before the last eruption, has always been treeless due to numerous avalanches in the winter season that kept the area in check. The Plains of Abraham were incredibly broad, stretching as far as our eyes could see, an endless sea of ash and rock. Traversing the barren, lifeless plain made us feel incredibly small. The immediate rising of the eastern side of the Helens served to put life into perspective.

During wildflower season, this section of the trail is one of the most floral and beautiful anywhere, with vibrant blooms carpeting the landscape and offering alternating views of the majestic Mount Adams, Hood, and Rainier. The air is filled with the sweet fragrance of wildflowers, creating a picturesque and serene environment. However, the final stretch was grueling. Our exhaustion was palpable, each step a reminder of the day's challenges. The heat was intense, beating down relentlessly on us, and the lack of water continued to take its toll on our energy levels, making each moment feel like an endurance test. Despite the beauty around us, the physical demands of the hike were undeniable.

The journey back to the car from the Plains of Abraham seemed to take only a fraction of the time. It always does. We were fortunate to encounter a few fresh springs, allowing us to enjoy some much-needed hydration.

After what felt like a blink of an eye, we reached the end of the trail and retraced our steps back to the car. The blazing sun had not been kind to us as we hiked, and the air-conditioned reprieve of the vehicle was a blessing as we drove back to civilization. Our legs ached and our clothes were drenched in sweat, but the sense of accomplishment overpowered our fatigue.

Our adventure concluded in the small town of Morton, where we found recovery at a local Mexican restaurant. The lively atmosphere and the smell of fresh cooked food greeted us as we entered. As we sat, sipping cool drinks and savoring hearty meals, we reflected on the day's journey. The tangy taste of the salsa and the rich flavors of the dishes brought a satisfying end to our strenuous day. We shared stories and laughter, realizing that the grueling hike had forged not just memories, but a stronger camaraderie among us.

As we enjoyed our early dinner, Dad couldn't resist sharing another one of his historical anecdotes, this time about the town of Morton. He leaned in and began, "Did you know that Morton is renowned for its annual Loggers' Jubilee?"

We listened attentively as he continued. "Every August, this small town comes alive with festivities, celebrating the rich logging heritage that has defined the region for over a century. The Logger's Jubilee has axe throwing, log rolling, and even tree climbing. It's a tribute to the hard working loggers and a fun way for the community to honor its history. If we ever find ourselves back here in late summer, we should definitely check it out."

His enthusiasm was infectious, prompting us to make a mental note to attend this unique event in the future. Dad's history lessons were always his way of coping with adversity. Despite my legs being battered and our severe exhaustion from the elements, there was something soothing in his resilient mindset.

The hike through Windy Pass was a testament to the raw beauty and harsh realities of nature. It reminded us of our own resilience and the bonds that strengthen in the face of adversity. The memories of the breathtaking views, the wildflowers, and the challenging terrain would stay with us forever, a story to be retold and cherished for years to come.

This hike also marked another portion of the Loowit trail checked off in our quest to circumnavigate the entire trail over time.

APE CANYON

STARTING OUR HIKE AT the Ape Canyon trailhead, my friend Ryan and I were excited for the adventure ahead. This was the one of the first hikes without my Dad as I was now in college, living over an hour south of my childhood home. Hiking the Loowit Trail was starting to shift to a mainly personal goal, not necessarily feeling the need to have Dad involved in each attempt. The trailhead this time was itself is a hidden gem, showing the effects on the non-blast side of

Mt. St. Helens. The hike begins with a gentle climb along the edge of a mudflow from the 1980 eruption before ending with a striking view of Ape Canyon at the beginning of the Plains of Abraham. Seeing the difference between the damaged mudflow area and the untouched trail shows the powerful impact of the eruption.

Ape Canyon is a narrowing gorge where the trail meets up with the start of the Plains of Abraham on its south side. It got its strange name from a local story about Bigfoot creatures. This tale goes back to July 1924, when a group of miners had a scary experience in the wilderness.

One night, as the miners settled into their rustic cabin, they were suddenly awakened by huge rocks falling all around them. They called the attackers "mountain devils" because it seemed like they were throwing stones with incredible aim. Filled with fear, the miners grabbed their guns and shot at the unseen attackers, which briefly stopped the rock-throwing. However, the assaults soon picked up again, creating a terrifying atmosphere.

In a chilling moment, one miner saw a Sasquatch reaching into the cabin through a hole, trying to grab an ax that was inside. Despite its strength, the creature couldn't pull the ax out, which only added to the miners' fears.

The frightening events continued throughout the night, keeping the miners on high alert until morning. When dawn finally broke, they cautiously left the cabin, still shaken. Fred Beck, one of the miners, reported seeing a Bigfoot creature at the edge of the canyon. In a moment of fear, he shot at it, horrified as the figure fell into the gorge.

This strange incident led to many theories over the years. Some believe the creatures might have been interdimensional beings, while others think local kids might have been playing pranks, throwing rocks at the cabin while their voices echoed, making them sound monstrous.

Today, the exact spot of the miners' cabin is still unknown, but Ape Canyon trail attracts hikers and adventurers because of its stunning beauty and rich history. The canyon remains a symbol of the wilderness's lasting appeal, inviting those brave enough to explore its depths and discover the incredible tales it holds.

As we started our climb, the trail was amazing, winding through old-growth forests so thick that we couldn't see the nearby mountain. Ryan and I joked around to keep our spirits up, making the journey even more fun.

We shared stories of past adventures and jokes, lightening our climb. "Remember that time we tried to hike to the Loowit trail from June Lake trailhead?" Ryan laughed, his voice echoing through the trees. "Yeah, and we ended up camping in the parking lot the night before experiencing a tropical storm," I replied, chuckling at the memory. We reminisced about the sudden storm, so severe that it washed away portions of the trail, and bonded over our love for exploration and the unpredictability of our adventures. While we couldn't complete the hike that time, it was a memorable experience, made even better by great company.

Each step felt like the forest was sharing its secrets with us, and the birds chirping provided a nice background to our conversation. Stories kept us motivated, and each step brought new waves of camaraderie and laughter. We paused now and then to take in the breathtaking views, the vast expanse of nature reminding us of the beauty beyond our daily lives. The journey was about both the destination and the experiences we shared along the way.

As we finally arrived at the end of the Ape Canyon trail, the sight before us was nothing short of breathtaking. Standing at the edge, we were greeted by a grand view that unfolded at the top of the narrow canyon, where downed trees lay scattered like ancient relics, telling tales of the past. The steepness of the canyon, combined with the strands of untouched Old Growth forest, created a stunning contrast. Ryan and I stood in awe, rendered speechless by the raw beauty surrounding us. We took a moment to pause, allowing the serenity of the landscape to wash over us, as we breathed in the fresh air and cherished the tranquility of this pristine sanctuary.

Now at the crossroads of the Ape Canyon trail and the Loowit Trail, I mentioned to Ryan the extraordinary view of the Plains of Abraham in which we were on the edge of. The vast landscape stretched out before us, with the harsh sun casting long shadows across the rugged terrain. I remembered my previous experience on this plain and shared it with Ryan, persuading him to explore further. We realized we had run out of water and. I suggested we look for water on the far side of the plain, hoping it was flowing even though it was early summer.

The plains were as surreal as I remembered, with endless stretches of pumice and volcanic ash shimmering in the heat. Remembering that the water on the far side was closer than returning to the car, we decided to continue despite our uncertainty.

As we began our journey across the Plains of Abraham, the ground was covered in pumice and volcanic ash. Each step we took stirred up ash, coating our skin with a dust-like layer that gradually began to scorch us. The plain seemed to go on forever with no end in sight. We kept moving forward, thinking of a spring fed creek that would give us water just behind Windy Pass. The dry, empty land seemed endless, but the hope of water kept us going. A light breeze would sometimes give brief relief, but the sun was relentless. We pushed on, driven by the thought of reaching the cool waters of the creek.

As we continued across the plains, the journey felt longer than we thought it would be. The horizon seemed to stretch out forever. Going through Windy Pass again, the shifting pumice tested our determination. The landscape was beautiful but harsh and uncaring. Earlier, we had been laughing and sharing stories, but now there was only silent determination. The only sounds were our footsteps on the volcanic soil and the wind whispering through the wilderness.

Navigating Windy Pass was as treacherous as I remembered, its rugged terrain relentless and unforgiving. The loose pumice and volcanic ash made every step a challenge, slipping beneath our feet with each movement. The path had not changed much since my last attempt, still demanding our utmost caution and focus. Surprisingly, hiking it in the opposite direction—uphill this time—proved a bit easier compared to the nerve-wracking decline my family experienced before. Despite the slight reprieve, the journey remained strenuous and required careful navigation to avoid any missteps on the unpredictable ground.

The water source that was expected to be there was dry. At this point, we were over five miles from the trailhead start and we discussed our options. After looking at the map, a few creeks showed up further upon the trail that made sense to investigate. The realization that we would need to continue on without immediate relief weighed heavily on our minds. However, the promise of water at those distant creeks pushed us to keep going. We knew we had to get water into us as soon as possible to sustain our energy, so we pressed forward with renewed determination, hoping that the next water source would not disappoint.

We reached the next creek on the map, but it was dry too. We felt the impact of having no water and it made things hard. We kept going towards the next creek, feeling down due to the dryness of the land. Each step felt heavier, not just from being tired, but from not knowing if we'd find water. Our mouths were dry and our energy was low, making us realize how serious our situation was. Still, we pushed on, hoping our efforts would pay off. As we moved, we watched the landscape closely, looking for any sign of water or a hidden spring that could save us. Finding water soon was crucial for our survival.

Eventually, after what felt like forever, we found the spring-fed creek in a small, green area filled with abounding willow trees surrounded by dry land. The sight of the clear, sparkling water brought us great relief. The cool water felt like a lifeline, giving us the energy we needed for the return hike back to the car. We took our time, enjoying each sip and splashing our faces, the water's cool touch washing away our tiredness.

As we sat by the creek, feeling the cool water rejuvenate our spirits, Ryan and I began to reflect on the craziness of this hike. What had originally been a straightforward trek had now doubled in distance due to our desperate search for water. We couldn't help but laugh at how unprepared we had been for such a grueling adventure, but the shared experience had also brought us closer. Each challenge we faced and overcame together made us appreciate the journey, no matter how tough it had been.

During our conversation, we couldn't help but draw parallels to the Israelites' journey out of Egypt. Their exodus was a long and arduous trek through the wilderness, fraught with its own perils and uncertainties. Just like us, they had faced numerous obstacles and moments when their faith and endurance were stretched thin. Yet, they kept moving forward, driven by the promise of reaching a land flowing with milk and honey.

The Israelites' journey was not just a physical one but also a profound stretching trust adventure. They endured countless hardships, from the harsh desert climate to the scarcity of food and water. Despite their dire circumstances, they continuously found reasons to trust in the divine guidance that led them. Their story is filled with moments of God's intervention, whether it was manna from heaven or water from a rock, reminding us that perseverance and faith can lead to unexpected miracles.

Reflecting on the Israelite's journey, Ryan and I found ourselves learning invaluable lessons. Their perseverance and trust in a higher plan resonated deeply with us as we navigated our own wilderness. Just as the Israelites had faced moments of despair, we too had our doubts and fears. But in those moments, we were reminded of the importance of hope, resilience, and faith. Each step we took towards finding water mirrored the Israelite's steps towards their Promised Land, reinforcing our understanding that sometimes, the journey itself holds more significance than the destination.

In our own lives, we often find ourselves in situations that test our resolve and challenge our spirits. The story of the Israelites serves as a timeless reminder that even in the face of insurmountable odds, the human spirit can prevail. Their unwavering belief in a better future, despite the trials they encountered, inspires us to keep striving towards our goals. The lessons we glean from their experiences can guide us through our personal struggles, providing a beacon of hope and a roadmap for resilience.

Trust in Him, whether the waters flow abundantly or the ground is dry as a bone. He always provides. Ryan and I were deeply grateful for the perspective charged conversation we had at an unexpected, remote willow spring. Despite the journey's hardships, this hike transformed into an incredible experience that would offer lessons for years to come.

Packing up from the spring, Ryan and I were ready to get back to the trailhead. As we packed up our gear, we started the long return to the car. The return journey felt quicker, maybe because we understood and appreciated each other more. There wasn't much to say; the experience itself told a story of strength and endurance.

Thinking back on the hike, we realized how important it is to have enough water. The adventure taught us a valuable lesson: always plan for the worst and make sure you have enough supplies. The beauty of the Plains of Abraham comes with its challenges, and being prepared is key to fully enjoying this amazing place. Each step we took through the tough but beautiful landscape reminded us of nature's power and the need to balance awe with respect, which is important for any true adventure.

This marked off the southeast portion of the Loowit trail in my quest to circumnavigate the mountain. Each attempt was becoming a source of adventures all in itself. As I ticked off each segment, I encountered new landscapes, each more memorable than the last. The trail was not just a physical journey but an emotional one as well, paving the way for personal growth. Each experience added a new chapter to my tale, reinforcing my connection with creation and deepening my appreciation for its unyielding beauty. Every challenging step taken on this path made the goal of completing the trail even more fulfilling.

SMITH CREEK

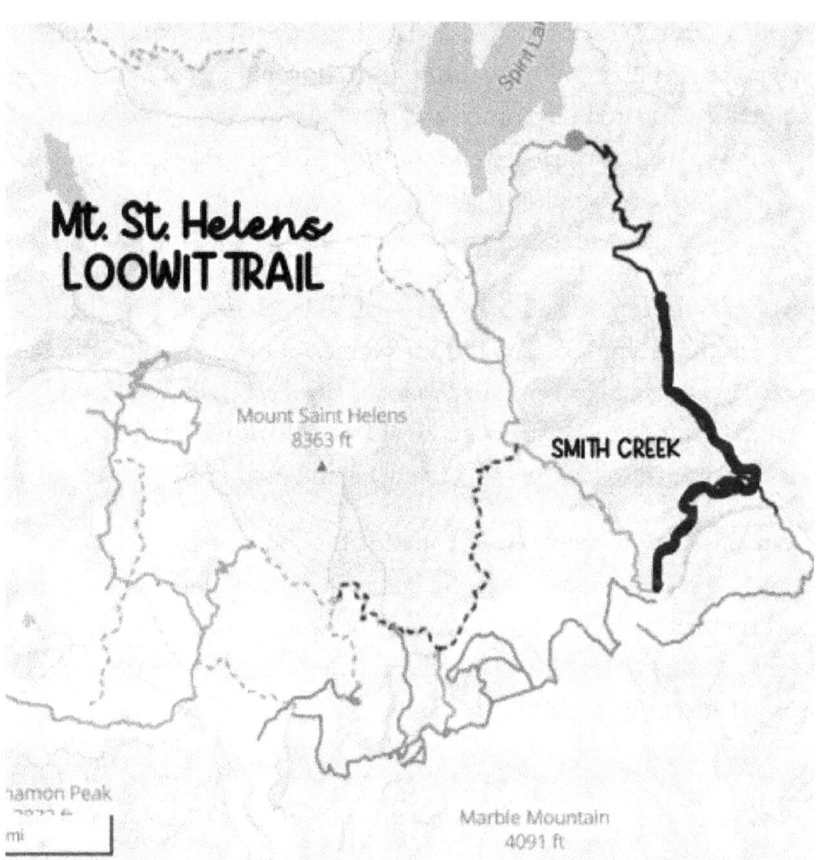

THE ADVENTURE TO SMITH Creek began with the exciting task of assembling a team of close friends: Dave, Nick, and Ryan. Each of us brought our unique personalities to the mix—Dave with his infectious enthusiasm and sense of humor, Nick with his meticulous planning and love for nature, and Ryan with his adventurous spirit and knack for storytelling. This combination made for a group that was never dull, always filled with laughter and camaraderie.

As we gathered to discuss our plans, our shared enthusiasm for the outdoors was palpable, fueling our anticipation for the journey ahead. The plan was to start at the lower Smith Creek trailhead, a scenic area we hadn't explored before, which added an extra layer of excitement to our outing. We envisioned a day filled with breathtaking views, challenging trails, and the thrill of trail running, punctuated by moments of shared adventure and new discoveries in the heart of nature. With our cars packed and spirits high, we were ready to embark on a memorable day of hiking and trail running.

My health had improved a lot since I started this journey around the Loowit Trail. I now had a regular schedule of running in the city, trail running in the Columbia River Gorge, and working out at home. Healthy eating and exercise made a big difference. Each day, I could go further, faster, and felt stronger. Health problems were fading away. I was determined to keep going. I knew I could do this.

We piled into my trusty 4x4, ready for the journey ahead. The drive along Forest Road 83 was smooth, but as we split off onto FR 8322, the road transformed. The once decent paved path turned into a bumpy, rugged gravel forest road, testing both the vehicle's capabilities and our sense of adventure.

"Hold on tight!" I called out, as the car jostled over rocks and deep ruts. The laughter from the backseat was infectious, turning what could have been a tedious ride into an enjoyable prelude to our hike. At one particularly rough stretch, Ryan decided to ride on the back of the SUV, a thrill seeking move that had us all in stitches. We even turned on the rear windshield wipers to add to the fun, each swipe met with cheers and shouts.

The condition of FR 8322 demanded a slow and steady approach. Potholes large enough to swallow a tire, loose gravel, and unexpected dips kept us vigilant. Despite the challenge, our spirits were high. The camaraderie and shared excitement about the adventure ahead kept everyone engaged.

After a painstakingly slow crawl in the vehicle, we finally reached the trailhead. The lower Smith Creek trailhead stood at the edge of the parking lot, inviting us to step into an unexplored wilderness. Our goal wasn't to tackle the Loowit Trail this time but to explore more of the Smith Creek and Lava Canyon area and experiment with trail running, a new challenge for our group.

Dave and Nick decided to hike up the Lava Canyon portion of the trail, a place I had been multiple times, filled with multiple waterfalls and extraordinary views. Their enthusiasm for the well-trodden path was evident, and I knew they would enjoy the panoramic views from the canyon's edge. Meanwhile, Ryan and I were eager to venture into the unknown, ready to explore the Smith Creek trail. With our trail running shoes laced tightly, we took off at a steady pace, the thrill of discovery propelling us forward.

My confidence in my hiking ability had grown, driving me to organize this trip. I felt ready to push boundaries and test my limits alongside friends who shared my passion for the outdoors. As we geared up and took our first steps on the trail, the anticipation of what lay ahead filled us with energy. Each of us carried a sense of curiosity and determination, prepared for whatever the day would bring.

Excited to start trail running along the Smith Creek trail, we said goodbye to Dave and Nick at our turn off. The air was crisp and refreshing as we began our run, but it wasn't long before we came across our first big challenge: the Muddy River. It stretched wide in front of us, with the remnants of an old bridge scattered across the riverbed, now just a few lonely pillars in the flowing water.

A frayed rope hung precariously down the crumbling riverbank, its support weakened by layers of ash and pumice deposited from past volcanic eruptions that had shaped the landscape over centuries. The remnants of volcanic activity were evident in the uneven terrain, with rough patches of hardened lava rock jutting out among the loose soil. We exchanged determined looks, prepped ourselves for the descent, and carefully made our way down the steep bank, where the loose dirt shifted beneath our feet, making each step feel treacherous. The air was thick with the smell of damp earth and the distant sound of rushing water filled our ears. Once at the bottom, we gazed at the formidable challenge ahead: crossing the wide riverbed, which appeared to stretch for hundreds of feet. The river's surface glistened under the sun, revealing a mix of smooth stones and swirling eddies that hinted at its current shallow depth and fast current.

The crossing wasn't easy. As we approached the river, the slippery rocks glistened ominously under the dappled sunlight, testing our balance with every cautious step. Each movement felt like a calculated risk, as we carefully assessed the stability of each stone to avoid an unfortunate fall into the fast waters below. Ryan and I worked closely together, our hands occasionally brushing against each other for support, and our shared struggle brought us even closer as we navigated the treacherous, slick ground.

After what felt like an eternity of careful maneuvering and focused determination, we finally reached the other side, overwhelmed with relief to find the trail mostly intact. To our surprise, this section of the path was remarkably well kept, with vibrant wildflowers lining the edges and the earthy scent of damp soil in the air, in much better shape than the bumpy road we had driven in on. It was a welcome sight that invigorated our spirits and made the arduous crossing worthwhile.

We continued for a short distance until the true nature of the Smith Creek trail started to show. The path wound through thick forest, giving us glimpses of the stunning beauty ahead. As we hiked for about half a mile soaking in the beauty and recovering from our Muddy River crossing, our conversation shifted to our upcoming half marathon. We talked about our training routines and our struggles with staying consistent while balancing life and fitness goals.

Determined to make the most of our time and embrace the beauty of nature, we decided to stick with our plan and started running on the trail again. The slight incline of the path provided just the right amount of challenge, guiding us along the stunning and picturesque riverbank of the Smith River, where the water sparkled like diamonds under the sun. The red rocks lining the river, with their rich hues and unique formations, made the landscape look almost like Mars, creating a surreal and otherworldly atmosphere that captivated our senses. As we continued, we marveled at the vibrant wildflowers dotting the edges of the path, adding splashes of color to the deep old growth forest that appeared around us. In the distance stood the silver trees—ghostly reminders of the eruption that had changed this place forever, their bare branches reaching skyward like skeletal fingers.

These striking silver trees are the charred remnants of the once lush forest that thrived in this area. Scorched by the intense, fiery blast of the volcano, they now stand as poignant symbols of nature's incredible resilience and strength, embodying both devastation and survival. Their haunting beauty adds a captivating, mysterious quality to our run, each tree standing like a sentinel against the vibrant greenery that is gradually reclaiming the land. As we jogged past, the silver bark glimmered in the sunlight, creating a stark yet beautiful contrast with the vivid hues of new and old growth. Each step we took among these remnants echoes the story of resilience and rebirth, making the experience all the more profound.

As we ran, the mix of red rocks and silver trees created a unique blend of colors and textures. The trail, while challenging, was incredibly rewarding, offering breathtaking views and a sense of achievement with every step. The journey along the riverbank was a testament to the power of nature and our determination to conquer the trail ahead.

Ryan and I maintained our steady pace, trail running along the picturesque Smith Creek trail. This path led us through a stunning mix of ancient old growth forest and newer growth closer to the gently flowing riverbanks, with each type of environment offering its own unique beauty and charm. The towering old growth trees stood majestically, their thick trunks and sprawling branches creating a magnificent canopy overhead. This natural shelter not only protected us from the harsh rays of the late Summer sun but also fostered a cool atmosphere that was perfect for an invigorating run.

As we navigated the trail, the ground beneath our feet was a mixture of soft pumice and rich dirt, which felt gentle yet sturdy, making every step a pleasure compared to the hard concrete of our usual urban runs. The forgiving surface cushioned our feet beautifully, allowing us to concentrate on our stride and rhythm rather than worrying about the impact on our joints.

With each mile, we embraced the sounds of nature—the gentle rustling of leaves, the distant call of birds, and the peaceful burbling of the river alongside us. We made excellent time, the trail encouraging our pace as we moved effortlessly under the sheltering trees, feeling a sense of freedom and connection to the great outdoors that is hard to replicate in the city. The experience was not just a workout; it was a revitalizing escape into nature, invigorating our spirits and deepening our appreciation for the beauty that surrounded us.

As we left the canopy of the forest and began running along the river itself, the scenery shifted dramatically. The trail followed the riverbed, offering stunning views of the water flowing beside us. The contrast between the lush greenery and the sparkling river was captivating, making each mile feel like a new adventure.

However, after about a mile of this riverbed run, the trail began to show signs of encroachment by new growth alder and willow trees. These young trees, while beautiful, made the path increasingly difficult to navigate. Overgrown sections forced us to slow down, turning our brisk run into a careful hike. Fallen trees and washouts added to the challenge, requiring us to clamber over obstacles and find new routes around blocked paths.

Realizing that the trail's condition wasn't improving despite our best efforts, we made the decision at mile six to turn around. We hoped to avoid keeping our friends Dave and Nick waiting too long at the trailhead, where they were likely enjoying the scenic views and fresh air. The return journey became a blend of running and hiking, as our earlier pace slowed considerably due to the need to carefully navigate the more challenging sections of the trail. The uneven terrain and occasional muddy patches required our full attention, forcing us to adjust our rhythm.

Despite the obstacles we encountered, the experience was incredibly rewarding. The combination of strenuous activity and breathtaking scenery not only challenged our bodies but also reinforced our love for trail running.

At this point in my hike journey around the Loowit trail, I noticed a change in how I approached the outdoors. My growing confidence and skills in navigating the challenging terrain of the blast zone allowed me to truly enjoy each experience in this beautiful mountain area. Running along the Smith Creek trail fueled my desire to finish the Loowit trail, as I became more comfortable with the unique challenges. The mix of rugged paths, stunning views, and my developing abilities energized me, turning what once felt intimidating into an exciting adventure. Every step felt like a celebration of nature's beauty and my growth as a trail enthusiast.

This trail running experience led me to complete three half marathon trail runs later in the year. Reflecting upon my journey from dealing with foot drop and constant overheating just a few years ago to now successfully handling intense situations felt like a tremendous accomplishment. Striding along those rugged paths, I embraced the challenges head-on, discovering newfound strength and resilience within myself. It was a remarkable departure from where I started, as each run not only tested my physical limits but also reinforced my determination and love for the outdoors. I was ready for anything, fueled by the memories of those early struggles and the satisfaction of overcoming them.

WORM FLOWS

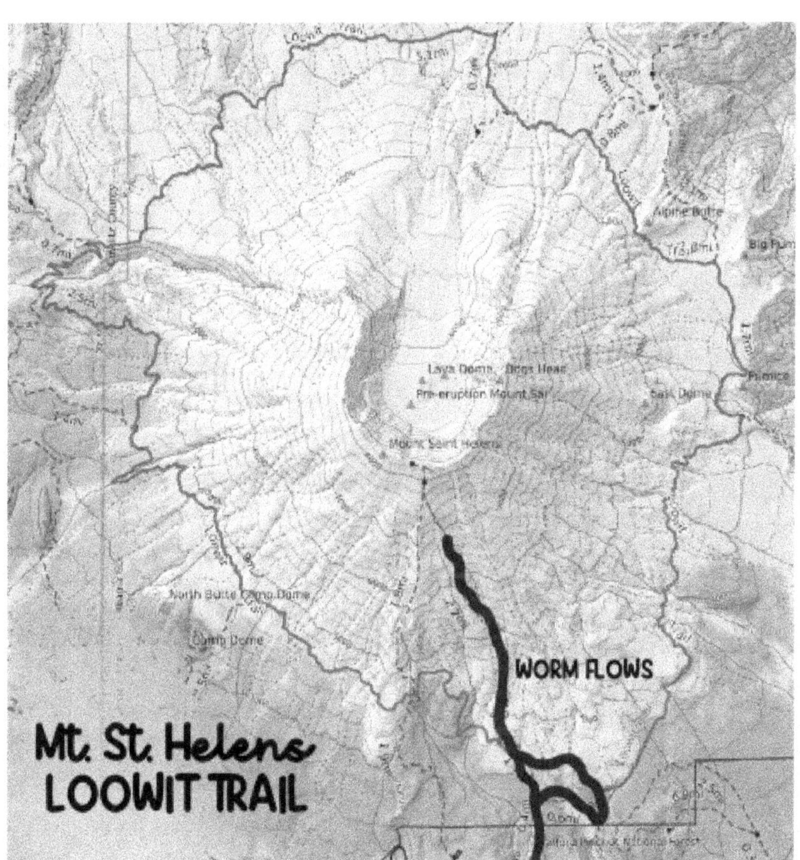

THE ANTICIPATION WAS through the roof as Ryan, Dave, and I prepared for our winter summit attempt of Mount St. Helens via the Worm Flows route. The morning was crisp and invigorating as we started from the Marble Mountain Sno-Park parking lot, our path marked by blue markers placed high to ensure we didn't lose our way in the season's heavy snow.

Ryan excitedly strapped a snowboard to his back, practically bouncing on his feet as he prepared to ride down the mountain after our arduous ascent. The thrill in his eyes and his infectious enthusiasm fueled our determination to embrace the exhilarating journey ahead. Dave, equally enthusiastic, joined in on the excitement, his energy radiating like sunlight and lifting the spirits of the entire group. We all felt the adrenaline coursing through our veins as we stood in the parking lot, ready for the next adventure.

However, deep inside, I was grappling with an internal battle that threatened to dim my own excitement. My health had taken an unexpected turn recently, leaving me with intense nerve pain radiating from my pelvic area whenever I engaged in any physical activity. Each movement seemed to amplify the discomfort, and the pain often triggered bouts of coughing that slowed me down significantly and stole my breath. Despite these daunting challenges, a fierce determination burned within me. I refused to let my struggles hold me back from experiencing the thrill of the mountain, and I was committed to pushing forward, hoping to enjoy even a fraction of the joy that Ryan and Dave radiated.

Ryan and Dave had become extremely close friends and steadfast supporters of me over the years. It was through their patient yet persistent encouragement to always push forward that our bond deepened. We all fed off each other's energy, and their presence bolstered my resolve in moments of doubt. I am incredibly grateful for these two souls; having them by my side instilled in me the confidence to face any challenge life throws my way. Support networks are a truly invaluable aspect of our journeys—never underestimate the strength and reassurance that stems from such connections.

As we strapped on our snowshoes and set off, the dense forest enveloped us, its towering trees providing a sense of both isolation and adventure. The snow crunched underfoot while my mind kept circling back to my health. The cold air and icy surroundings seemed like a blessing, helping to keep my body from overheating and potentially easing my symptoms.

We trekked through the forest, gradually witnessing the landscape transform into a breathtaking winter wonderland. The branches, heavy with fresh snow, bowed gracefully under their weight, creating a picturesque scene that felt both tranquil and challenging. Each crunch of snow beneath our boots was a test of endurance, but the beauty of the trail and the thrill of the ascent kept our spirits high.

As we ventured deeper, we finally arrived at the first meadow, a stunning opening in the winter forest. The sight was so inviting that we couldn't resist the urge to take a break. With laughter echoing through the trees, we engaged in an impromptu snowball fight. Snow flew in all directions as we playfully ducked and dodged, savoring the joy of the moment. After a spirited battle, we resumed our trek, invigorated and ready to tackle the next challenge on our journey.

The route itself is renowned for its breathtaking views and demanding terrain, making it a favorite among seasoned climbers and outdoor enthusiasts. Starting at an elevation of about 2,800 feet, the Worm Flows route takes climbers past the stunning Chocolate Falls, a seasonal waterfall that gracefully cascades along the banks of Swift Creek, creating a picturesque scene that captivates all who pass. The sound of the water rushing down the rocks adds to the experience, providing a refreshing ambiance.

As climbers continue on their journey, the path transitions into a stark and barren landscape characterized by mudflows and rocky outcrops, which serve as a reminder of the area's geological history. Wooden cairn poles line the trail, expertly guiding adventurers as they ascend towards the seismic station, which sits at an impressive altitude of 6,200 feet.

On clear days, the summit reveals dramatic panoramic views of the majestic peaks of Washington and Oregon, including the iconic Mount Rainier, Hood, and the rugged Cascade Range. This breathtaking vista serves as a reward for those who endure the challenging climb, inspiring many to push their limits and fully immerse themselves in the beauty of nature. Whether taking photos or simply pausing to soak in the scenery, climbers often find this experience to be a highlight of their outdoor pursuits.

Lost in my thoughts on the trail we had committed to, I found solace in the rhythmic pattern of our snowshoeing. The snow-covered ground felt forgiving compared to urban pavement, cushioning each step. Yet, the nerve pain lingered, a persistent reminder of my limits. I knew pushing myself could lead to more coughing fits, but I was resolved to enjoy this adventure with my friends.

As we pressed on, the forest began to thin, revealing an expansive snow-covered landscape that stretched out before us. It was evident that we were traversing what was likely a lava field, then ascending a treeless slope toward the summit. The incline was becoming noticeably steeper. The southern flank of Mount St. Helens loomed ahead, and despite my health challenges, I felt a surge of determination. The journey promised to be demanding, but with Ryan and Dave by my side, I was prepared to confront whatever lay ahead.

As we climbed to elevations between 5,500 and 6,000 feet, the ascent became noticeably tougher. Ryan seemed to be struggling, though I had a feeling he might be exaggerating his effort to make me feel better about my own condition. Dave stayed close by my side, offering support as my pace slowed considerably.

The deeper we ventured into the climb, the more frequent my bouts of coughing became. Each step felt heavier than the last, my body protesting against the physical exertion. The nerve pain flared up, sending sharp jolts throughout my body, making the hike even more grueling. We found ourselves stopping to rest more often, trying to manage the growing fatigue and discomfort.

It was disheartening to realize we were only halfway along the trail and that I likely wouldn't be able to finish the climb. Despite my determination, my body had its limits, and those limits were becoming painfully clear. Dave's presence was comforting, but the weight of disappointment hung over me.

Meanwhile, Ryan was finding ways to enjoy the snow despite the challenge. He took breaks from the climb to snowboard down the gullies along the trail, his laughter echoing through the crisp mountain air. His lightheartedness was a stark contrast to my own struggle, yet it reminded me of the joy and adventure we sought in this journey.

With every step, the battle to summit Mount St. Helens grew more arduous. My health condition wasn't giving me any reprieve, but I was determined to push as far as I could. Dave and I continued our slow progress, motivated by the thought of Ryan's triumphant snowboarding and the camaraderie that brought us here.

My thoughts on this hike drew a powerful parallel to the story of Moses leading the Israelites through the Wilderness. Much like our arduous journey up Mount St. Helens, Moses and the Israelites faced immense physical and emotional challenges during their grueling 40 years in the wilderness. They endured relentless hardships such as hunger, thirst, and a constant test of faith and endurance that pushed their limits. Each day was a struggle, as they wandered through barren landscapes, longing for the home they had been promised.

Just as my friend Dave remained steadfast by my side throughout the hike, Aaron provided vital support to Moses during crucial moments when he grew weary and burdened by the weight of leadership. For instance, during the battle against the Amalekites, when Moses could no longer keep his arms raised in prayer, Aaron stepped in to hold his arms aloft. This act of solidarity was instrumental in ensuring the Israelite's victory. It highlighted the importance of community and support, reminding me that we often rely on others to uplift us during our most challenging times.

Both our trek and the Israelite's journey were filled with moments of doubt and frustration. The Israelites frequently questioned whether they would ever reach the Promised Land, voicing their fears and uncertainties as they faced obstacles along the way. Similarly, I found myself grappling with self-doubt, wondering if I could complete my climb to the summit above the Loowit Trail on the mountain's south side. Those moments of vulnerability were part of the experience, reflecting the human condition of seeking assurance and strength during times of struggle.

Ryan's moments of joy, punctuated by laughter and spontaneous snowboarding, reminded me of the celebrations and expressions of faith that the Israelites shared. They celebrated significant milestones, such as crossing the Red Sea safely and receiving manna from heaven, which served as a reminder of hope and divine provision. Each cheer and shared experience on the mountain felt like a small celebration, reinforcing our collective spirit and determination.

The ultimate goal of reaching the summit felt akin to the Promised Land that the Israelites were striving toward, a beacon of hope on the horizon even when the journey was fraught with hardships and seemed almost unattainable at times. This comparison beautifully emphasized themes of perseverance, unwavering support, faith, and resilience in the face of daunting challenges. Just as the Israelites had to keep moving forward despite their fears, we too had to push through the fatigue and uncertainty to reach our own summit, finding strength in each other and in our shared purpose.

Dave and I finally stopped. I could go no further until I rested. We decided to have an impromptu lunch, using the time to eat and fill up on water. The mood was somber, and though conversation might have occurred, my mind was elsewhere. Battling back and forth in my mind, I ultimately decided, with Dave's gentle but firm encouragement, to turn around.

"Hey," Dave said, breaking the silence. "You've come extremely far, you know. That's something to be really proud of."

I nodded, appreciating his words but feeling the sting of disappointment. Just then, Ryan rejoined us, and we collectively agreed to turn back at an elevation of 6,250 feet, short of the 8,365 foot summit. Ryan strapped on his snowboard and, before we knew it, was gliding down the slopes, his figure quickly becoming a dot in the distance. Dave and I were left to make our return together.

The descent was not as strenuous as the climb, and I found the intense coughing nearly stopped. However, we still found ourselves pausing several times along the way back. Usually, the hike back feels shorter, but this one seemed just as long, adding to my frustration.

Finally, exhaustion took over. "I can't go any further," I whined, the electrical shock sensations from the nerve pain beating me down physically.

Dave, witnessing my continued struggle and with his patience stretching thin, told me he would be right back. A couple of minutes later, he returned with good news. "We're less than 1,000 feet from the parking lot. We've made it."

With Dave's help, I managed the last stretch, and we emerged at the parking lot to see Ryan smiling beside his snowboard. We packed everything back into the car, and during the drive home, we had some bonding time. Both Ryan and Dave jumped in to encourage me, shifting my mentality from defeat to success. Despite the challenges, I was impressed by how far I had come. This was a win.

TOUTLE RIVER

MY DAD AND I ARRIVED at the Blue Lake trailhead, feeling excited and ready to embark on our adventure through the Sheep Canyon loop, part of the Loowit Trail, and the beautiful Blue Lake trail. The west side of Mt. St. Helens was an area rich in ecological diversity and geological history. This region is marked by the contrast of immense old growth forests standing resiliently alongside the decimated gulleys created by the dramatic river run-off from the Toutle

River. This river plays a vital role in the area's ecosystem, supporting wildlife and plant life that have reclaimed the landscape after the 1980 eruption. Each step on the trail deepened our appreciation for this remarkable environment and fueled our desire to complete the entire Loowit Trail.

As we stepped out of the car, the fresh mountain air filled our lungs, and we couldn't help but take a moment to soak in the stunning surroundings. The first thing that caught our attention was the wide floodplain stretching before us, a stark reminder of the powerful floods that had reshaped this landscape over the years. It was fascinating to think about how nature had carved this area, creating a mix of beauty and challenges.

As we began our hike, we noticed the washout area was strewn with pumice, creating a challenging start to our journey. The rocky terrain crunched under our boots, and with every step, we felt the excitement of the adventure ahead. However, navigating through this rocky expanse proved to be tricky. We struggled to identify the trail amidst the scattered pumice and uneven ground. The remnants of past washouts added to the unpredictability of the terrain, making us feel like explorers on a quest to uncover the way forward. Each step felt like a mini-adventure as we worked together to find our path. I was glad to be on a hike with Dad once again. It had been too long since we had hiked last.

Determined to reach Blue Lake, we pressed on despite the obstacles. The trail became increasingly difficult, winding through areas where the vegetation had taken over, obscuring our view of the path. Thick willow trees seemed to reach out at us amongst the ravines of pumice, but we were determined not to let them deter us. Each moment we spent navigating through the wild was filled with anticipation, and even though it was challenging, it made us feel more connected to the wilderness around us.

As we continued our journey, we could hear birds chirping and flow of Coldspring Creek on the edge of the flood plain. We took a few breaks to catch our breath, using these moments to appreciate the beauty of the forest. The trees towered off in the distance above what would become Blue Lake, their branches swaying softly. We knew that reaching Blue Lake would be a small feat, but the thought of getting there fueled our determination nevertheless.

Coldspring Creek marked the edge of the pumice plain. We could see what appeared to be a service road for what lay at the end of it—the former trailhead miles further ahead. This flood washout had forced the Forest Service to redo the trailhead. We turned and headed towards Blue Lake, following Coldspring Creek where the sound of the water splashing over stones created a soothing backdrop as we trekked onward. The path alongside the creek was more forgiving, offering us a brief respite from the rugged terrain we had encountered. The closer we got to Blue Lake, the more our excitement grew, spurred on by the rhythmic flow of the creek guiding our way.

When we finally approached Blue Lake, it felt like a monumental achievement despite the relatively short distance from the car. The trail ahead was obscured by thick groves of alders and willows, making visibility nearly impossible. We pushed through the dense vegetation, our progress slow but steady. With each step, the anticipation grew. The closer we got, the more the landscape seemed to close in around us, almost as if it were testing our resolve to continue. We exchanged encouraging words, knowing that we were in this together.

After the unexpected trek so far, we stepped out of the trees and onto the shore of Blue Lake. It was a welcome sight. The lake's serene blue waters stood in stark contrast to the rugged terrain we had just traversed. It felt like stepping into a different world, one that was peaceful and calm. Surrounded by the forest that had survived the 1980 eruption, we were greeted by a tranquil oasis amidst the chaos of nature. Carpets of white flowers covered much of the ground leading to the shore, adding to the mesmerizing beauty of the area. As we sat by the lake, we took a moment to appreciate everything we had accomplished and the stunning beauty that surrounded us. It was a day we would never forget, filled with adventure, perseverance, and the beauty of nature.

We settled by the lake for a brief respite, soaking in the beauty of our surroundings with my Dad. Usually, we would linger longer at a picturesque spot like this, but our itinerary was packed with adventure today. After a moment of reflection and a quick snack, we knew it was time to move on. With a shared glance, we acknowledged the need to keep pushing forward. We began our trek back along Coldspring Creek, retracing our steps towards a crossing we had previously spotted. A trailsign loomed ahead, guiding us towards the rest of the trail that would lead us around the loop of Sheep Canyon, promising more breathtaking views and discoveries.

Crossing Coldspring Creek marked the start of a new challenge. On the other side lay a steep hillside covered in towering old growth forest, a stark contrast to the rugged floodplain we had just navigated. To cross the creek, we needed to traverse a downed log that swayed slightly with the current. My Dad went first, steadying the log as best he could.

"Take it slow," he said, extending his hand to help me across.

With his support, I carefully made my way over. Despite my health being on the mend from my previous nerve pain, the crossing tested my balance and resolve. Each step was deliberate, my foot cautiously finding stability on the moving log. But I was determined to embrace this trail and not worry about holding my Dad back. My resolve pushed me onward, step by step, until we both stood on the other side, ready for the next hurdle.

Scaling the fifteen foot steep hillside that followed was daunting. The incline seemed almost vertical in places, and thoughts of doubt crept in—could I really make it up this slope? The earth was loose beneath our feet, and grabbing onto roots or rocks for support was essential. But with my Dad's encouragement, I took it one step at a time. He was always there, offering a hand when needed, reminding me to focus on each small victory.

"You're doing great," he'd say, his voice steady and reassuring.

Finally reaching the top, we were greeted by the remnants of rustic campsites scattered along the trail. Fire rings and flattened patches of ground hinted at past adventurers who had paused here to rest. We made a mental note to return someday and give one of these spots a proper stay. The serene beauty of the area was captivating, with beautiful views of the lake below us as we began this part of the trail.

The forest we entered seemed untouched by the eruption. Towering ancient trees surrounded us, their thick trunks and sprawling branches creating a canopy that filtered the sunlight into a soft, dappled glow. The scent of evergreen bows filled the air, and the soil underfoot was cushioned by decades of fallen needles.

Walking through this pristine landscape felt like stepping into a different world—a world where nature continued its cycles undisturbed. The trail here was well-trodden, a clear path through this timeless forest, evidence of many hikers who had come before us. Each step forward reinforced the bond between my Dad and me. The challenges we faced together and the beauty we shared along the way transformed this hike into an unforgettable journey.

As we continued, the trail offered stunning vistas of the lake below. The water shimmered in the sunlight, framed by the dense foliage that lined the shore. The tranquility of the scene was a stark contrast to the rugged terrain we had conquered earlier. It was moments like these that made the effort worthwhile.

The forest looked as if no eruption had ever occurred. Very old trees stood tall, their bark weathered but strong. The trail seemed very well traveled, a ribbon of dirt winding through the landscape. The sounds of birds chirping and leaves rustling created a peaceful soundtrack to our hike.

Occasionally, we would come across signs of wildlife—tracks in the mud, a flash of movement in the underbrush. These glimpses of the animals that called this place home added to the sense of wonder.

Our conversation ebbed and flowed naturally, sometimes filled with stories and laughter, other times quiet as we absorbed the experience. My Dad shared anecdotes from his past hikes, each story adding a layer of richness to our adventure. His love for the outdoors was evident in every word, and it deepened my appreciation for the journey we were on.

By the time we reached a clearing with a panoramic view of the surrounding mountains, any doubts I had about my ability to keep up had melted away. The sense of accomplishment was overwhelming. We stood there for a while, taking it all in, feeling connected to each other and the natural world around us.

Every part of the trail told a story of resilience and renewal. From the towering old growth trees to the vibrant wildflowers dotting the landscape, each element was a testament to nature's enduring strength. This hike with my Dad through the Toutle River area was more than just a physical journey—it was a journey of the heart, one that strengthened our bond and left us with memories to cherish once more.

As we walked, the landscape around us began to change, signaling our approach to Sheep Canyon. The Toutle Trail intersected with the Sheep Canyon Trail here, which climbed the mountain on the south side of the canyon up to the Loowit Trail. We decided to stay on the Toutle and made our way across Sheep Canyon via a scenic footbridge. The bridge offered stunning views into the canyon below, where the rugged terrain met a serene ribbon of water flowing peacefully.

This area at the footbridge was absolutely stunning. A very large waterfall graced the canyon just downstream of us, its powerful cascade creating a mesmerizing symphony of rushing water that echoed off the canyon walls. Of course, we took the opportunity to do a side exploration, eagerly capturing tons of pictures to document this beautiful moment. My fear of heights prompted my Dad and I to stay away from the erosion prone edges. We settled down on a large, flat rock near the footbridge, unpacking our lunch and enjoying a delicious meal amid the grandeur of nature. As we ate, we shared stories and laughed, the sound of the water providing a soothing backdrop to our heartfelt conversation. This pause allowed us to truly soak in the beauty around us, making the experience even more memorable.

Continuing on towards the South Fork Toutle River with our bellies full, the trail became less maintained. Fallen logs blocked our path, requiring us to step over obstacles and duck under low hanging branches. Despite the challenges, the beauty of the surroundings made every effort worthwhile. After about one and a half miles, we reached the junction of the Toutle Trail and the Loowit Trail at the edge of the South Fork Toutle River's canyon.

This wide canyon bore the scars of Mount St. Helen's eruption. The rapid melting of the mountain's glaciers had sent a massive mudslide down the valley. Now, the river was a small ribbon of water winding through the expansive canyon. The contrast between the narrow stream and the vast, open space left by the mudslide was striking.

We turned right onto the Loowit Trail and began climbing along the west side of the mountain. As we ascended, we left the dense forest behind and entered the blast zone—an area where trees had not survived the eruption. The landscape here was open, offering increasingly spectacular views of Mount St. Helen's rim. To the north, the top of Mount Rainier peeked over the horizon, a majestic sight against the clear blue sky.

The trail was surrounded by wildflowers, taking full advantage of the clearings created by the blast. We passed through vibrant stands of bear grass and encountered large numbers of orange tiger lilies, purple penstemon, red columbine, paintbrush, and various colors of phlox. Each flower added a splash of color to the otherwise stark terrain, showcasing nature's resilience and ability to reclaim and renew.

Patches of snow lingered in gullies along the way, remnants of the previous winter. The trail eventually leveled out and continued traversing the mountain's western flank. We dipped in and out of the tree line, passing through a variety of landscapes—each offering its own unique beauty and challenges.

As we hiked along the trail, I couldn't help but reflect on how much I had overcome to reach this point. Each step felt like a testament to my determination, with the Loowit Trail revealing its unique character section by section. From the north, east, south and now on the west, I was conquering not just the terrain, but also my own limits. It was breathtaking to witness how the landscape transformed with each quadrant; the eruption's devastating force had sculpted the land in such varied ways, particularly along the north, where the scars were the most pronounced. Yet, here I was, in the midst of nature's resilience, marveling at how beauty can emerge from such chaos.

As we continued, the trail led us back to the Sheep Canyon Trail. The return loop trail started to decline, and soon we began hearing odd noises echoing through the forest. My Dad seemed to recognize them but didn't say a word. His pace quickened, and his eyes held a spark of determination.

"What are those sounds?" I asked, curiosity bubbling inside me.

Dad just smiled, urging me forward. "You'll see soon enough," he said, his tone teasing yet filled with excitement.

The mystery only heightened my interest. As I caught up to Dad, he finally revealed the source of the sounds. "Those are elk calls," he said, a grin spreading across his face. "Herds are starting to recover in this area after the blast."

Elk. The thought electrified me. I had to see them. Fueled by anticipation, I broke into a run without even a second thought. The sudden burst of energy caught my Dad off guard. He wasn't much of a runner, so he let me go ahead, trusting my eagerness.

"Be careful!" he called after me, his voice fading as I sped down the trail.

I dashed through the woodland, my feet pounding the dirt path. The sounds grew louder, more distinct, urging me onward. I veered slightly off the trail, navigating through the dense foliage in my quest to catch a glimpse of these majestic creatures.

And then, through a break in the trees, I saw them—down the hill, moving gracefully through the underbrush. I paused for a moment, watching in awe. They seemed almost ethereal, their movements fluid and powerful.

Determined to get even closer, I sprinted down the hill, my heart racing not just from the exertion but from the sheer thrill of the encounter. By the time I reached the spot where they had been moments before, I caught another glimpse of them. This time, they were on the opposite side of the river valley, having crossed the Toutle River and ascended an even steeper incline.

I stood there, amazed. In the brief span of minutes, these incredible animals had covered ground that would take me hours to traverse. The steep decline, the river crossing, the rapid ascent—they tackled it all with effortless grace. Their presence was a testament to nature's resilience and adaptability.

As I watched them disappear into the forest, I felt a deep sense of respect and admiration. These elk were more than just survivors; they were symbols of the wild's enduring spirit. The sight of them moving so swiftly and elegantly through such challenging terrain left an indelible mark on me.

When I finally made my way back to the trail and found my Dad waiting for me, I could barely contain my excitement.

"I saw them, Dad! They were amazing!" I exclaimed, breathless but exhilarated.

He smiled, his eyes twinkling with shared joy. "I knew you'd love it."

As we continued our hike back towards Blue Lake and the car, the memory of the elk stayed with me. It was a fitting end to an already unforgettable journey. The landscape we had explored—the old growth forests, the blast zone, the wildflower strewn trails—was alive with stories of renewal and survival.

We soon arrived at a campground near the footbridge that we had overlooked on our way in. This area was truly remarkable, surrounded by towering trees and offering breathtaking views of the landscape. It was a peaceful oasis, brimming with life—a perfect spot for a future camping trip. We took a moment to explore, adding this campground to our list of must visit places. The thought of spending a night here, under the stars and enveloped by natural beauty, was simply too tempting to resist.

From the campground, we turned left and began our journey back on the Blue Lake Trail. The trail that had seemed so challenging on the way in now offered a pleasant downhill trajectory. We relished the easier descent, our spirits lifted by the day's experiences and the knowledge that we were heading home.

Knowing all the ins and outs of crossing Coldspring Creek and navigating the washout past Blue Lake made our return journey swift. Each step felt more confident as we retraced our route, familiar landmarks guiding us along the way. The creek crossing, which had initially tested our resolve, was now a straightforward task. The washout, with its rocky terrain, seemed less daunting, and we moved across it with ease.

It had been a full day, filled with physical challenges and breathtaking sights of over 10 miles. As we neared the trailhead, both Dad and I could feel the satisfying exhaustion that comes from a day well spent. Despite the demanding hike, I was impressed with how my health had held up. The sense of accomplishment was immense.

Finally reaching the car, we took a moment to reflect on our adventure. Climbing into the seats, we shared smiles of triumph. Another hike crossed off our list, and what a memorable one it had been.

"That trail was one for the books," my Dad said, eyes gleaming with satisfaction.

I nodded in agreement, replaying the day's highlights in my mind—the serene moments by Blue Lake, the exhilarating encounter with the elk, the awe-inspiring landscapes we had traversed. Each memory was a testament to the journey's impact on us.

As we drove home, the conversation flowed easily, filled with plans for future hikes and the promise of many more adventures to come. The Toutle River trail had given us more than just a physical challenge; it had strengthened our bond and left us with stories to cherish for years to come.

The drive back was smooth, the miles slipping away as we relived our day. The setting sun painted the sky in shades of orange and pink, a beautiful end to an extraordinary journey. As we pulled into our driveway, there was a shared understanding that this hike was just the beginning of many more to come.

The experience had deepened our appreciation for the natural world and reminded us of the joys of exploration. With each step, we had forged memories that would last a lifetime, and we knew that the next trail awaited, ready to offer its own unique wonders.

SASQUATCH STEPS

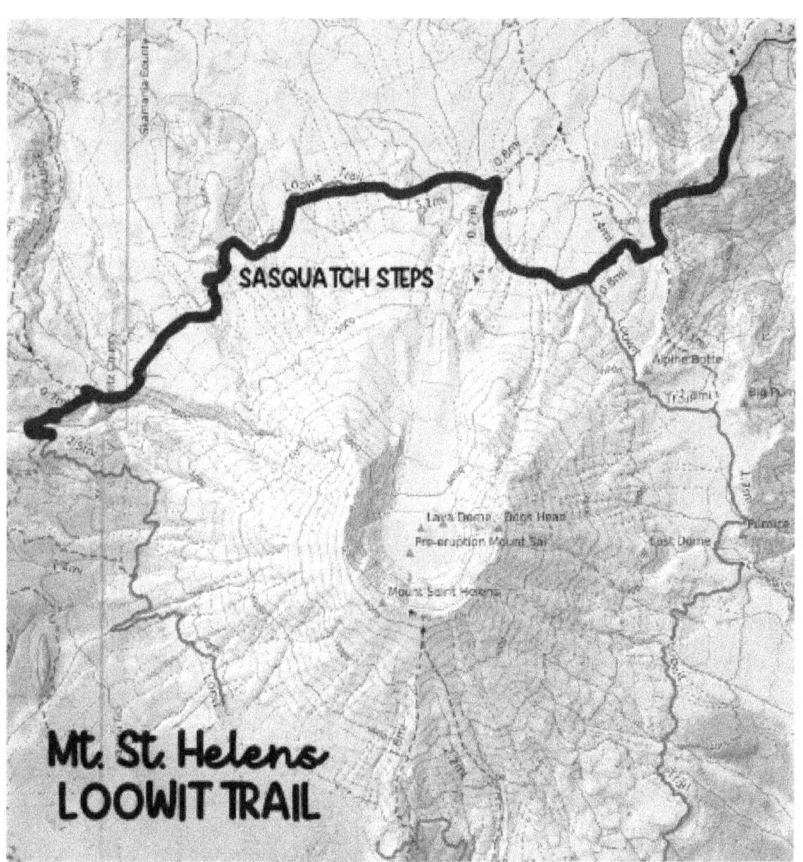

AS THE WEEKEND DREW near, I found myself caught in a whirlwind of emotions, a blend of excitement and nervousness swirling within me. The plan we had devised was nothing short of ambitious: to circumnavigate Mount St. Helens in just two days. We would start from the Windy Ridge Parking lot and hike counterclockwise around the mountain. Initially, a group of my friends had eagerly signed up for this adventure, each one expressing enthusiasm about the journey ahead. However, as the departure date approached, one by one, they began to drop out, each citing different reasons—work commitments that couldn't be postponed, family obligations that needed their attention, and unexpected events that popped up out of nowhere.

By the time Friday rolled around, it was just me and Shelly, a friend from church. Although we had known each other for a while, we weren't particularly close, which added to my apprehension about spending two whole days together on a demanding hike. Still, we both felt a strong determination to see the adventure through, ready to tackle whatever challenges lay ahead.

Early Saturday morning, with the sun barely peeking over the horizon, we set off from Vancouver. The drive to Windy Ridge took a few hours, but the journey felt even longer due to the initial awkwardness that hung in the air between us. It was a strange feeling, driving toward an adventure without the familiar chatter of close friends. As we left the city behind, the urban landscape gradually transformed into the lush greenery of the Pacific Northwest. Towering evergreens lined the highway, their dark silhouettes standing tall against the brightening sky above. As we passed through small towns and navigated winding roads, the scenery around us became more rugged and wild, each mile drawing us closer to our destination.

At first, our conversation was slow, filled with polite exchanges and nervous laughter as we tried to break the ice. But as the miles rolled by, we began to relax and open up, sharing stories about our lives and our expectations for the hike ahead. The anticipation in the car was palpable; both of us could feel the excitement building as we left the routine of daily life behind. We were eager to escape our usual surroundings and embrace the challenge that awaited us, ready to forge a bond over the shared experience of venturing on the Loowit Trail.

As we drove on, I couldn't help but think about the beauty and unpredictability of the journey we were about to embark on. With every twist and turn of the road, I felt my excitement grow, hoping that this adventure would not only test our physical limits but also strengthen our mental toughness in unexpected ways. The multiple short attempts at completing sections of the trail left this grand finale, I wanted to do the trail in its entirety.

As we made our way through the Gifford Pinchot National Forest, the air around us shifted, becoming noticeably cooler and crisper. The towering trees formed a dense canopy above, but every once in a while, it opened up just enough for us to catch glimpses of the majestic Mount St. Helens standing proudly in the distance. Each time we spotted the mountain, a wave of awe washed over us, its snow-capped peak glistening beautifully in the morning light, almost as if it were inviting us to explore its wonders.

Finally, we reached the Windy Ridge Parking Lot, which would serve as the starting point for this adventure. As I stepped out of the car, I took a deep, refreshing breath, savoring the cool mountain air filling my lungs. I glanced over at Shelly, and we shared a look that spoke volumes—a mix of excitement, anticipation, and determination gleamed in our eyes. We knew we had a long journey ahead of us, but the breathtaking beauty of the landscape and the promise of adventure reignited our spirits and propelled us forward.

Little did we realize at that moment that this hike would not only test our physical limits more than anything we had experienced up until this point but it would also create lasting memories, good or bad. With our backpacks securely strapped on we embarked on the Loowit Trail, ready to take the first steps. Each step was a commitment to conquering challenges together, and as we left the parking lot, the anticipation of what lay ahead filled us with an exhilarating sense of purpose.

Starting our departure from Windy Ridge, we made our way towards the pumice plain. The landscape opened up to reveal breathtaking views of Mt. Adams, with occasional glimpses of Mt. Rainier peeking through the horizon. This segment of the trail felt all too familiar to me, a place where countless excursions over the years had filled my memories. The pumice, ash, and relentless sun were there once again, casting a harsh yet awe inspiring beauty across the terrain.

As we made our way to the pumice plain, we maintained a steady pace across the dry plateau, which lacked any water once again. Every streambed we encountered was parched, but that didn't stop us. Learning the lesson the hard way from previous hikes, we were well stocked with water. We focused on reaching the South Fork Toutle River, our planned campsite for the night, where we could enjoy easy access to water—one of only two guaranteed water sources on the Loowit Trail this time of year.

During the beginning of our hike, Shelly opened up about her fascinating background. Raised by missionary parents in the remote regions of Papua New Guinea, she had witnessed a world vastly different from most. She shared haunting stories of cannibalism through the innocent lens of a child, making the hair on the back of my neck stand up. As our conversation shifted, she talked about her journey to med school and her college life in southern Israel, near the Gaza border. Frequent siren raids and the constant threat of danger seemed to have become a natural part of her life. At one point, her phone buzzed with a warning to shelter in place due to a rocket—an eerie reminder of the world she had come from.

Shelly went on to share a time when she journeyed to neighboring Jordan and explored a trail among the gullies, reminiscent of the one we were currently hiking. My mind reeled as she recounted the experience of local men following her, armed and seemingly unyielding. Yet, she didn't appear to fear for her life even as the daylight faded. Instead, I learned how resourceful she was in those moments; she managed to communicate with one of her friends who sent her directions, ultimately rescuing her from what could have been a dangerous situation. I was beginning to realize that this wasn't just another friend from church. Shelly had a remarkably unique background and was well on her way to becoming a doctor. Wow, did I hit the jackpot with this hiking partner.

We stopped where the turnoff to Loowit Falls was. My memories drifted back to the first time I saw this waterfall up close with my Dad. What a great memory to relish in—the rushing water, the cool mist on our faces, and the sense of wonder that always accompanied our adventures together. As I lost myself in those nostalgic thoughts, I noticed that Shelly had decided to take her shoes off. Feeling constricted, she wanted to go the rest of the hike barefoot. Oh my... her bravery brought a smile to my face; I admired her spontaneous spirit. Watching her carefully navigate the pumice and washout terrain reminded me of the freedom that comes with embracing the natural world, unencumbered by the limits we often impose on ourselves.

As we pressed on, our pace quickened as we approached the Sasquatch Steps, or known as just the Steps. The gusty plain stretched out before us, a vast expanse that seemed to go on forever, dotted with washed-out gullies that bore the scars of winter's relentless runoff. The wind howled fiercely around us, infusing our journey with a wild, raw energy that made every step feel more alive. We navigated the challenging terrain, weaving our way around obstacles, while the majestic north slope of Mount St. Helens loomed ever closer, guiding us toward our destination.

Eventually, we reached the heart of the blast zone, a place that seemed both otherworldly and humbling. Here, the trail cut directly through the path of the volcanic breach, offering breathtaking views into the remaining crater that held the secrets of nature's fury. The solitude of this landscape was striking; it was hard to believe that we hadn't encountered another hiker in over an hour, and by the looks of it, we wouldn't for the rest of our trip. It felt as though we had the entire blast zone to ourselves, a unique experience that was both eerie and exhilarating.

I paused for a moment, allowing myself to take in the stunning surroundings. The vast emptiness stretched out around me, and the surreal landscape, sculpted by unimaginable forces, seemed to tell a story of destruction and rebirth. Standing in the middle of this desolate beauty, I felt a deep sense of wonder as I tried to grasp the scale of the devastation that had shaped this land. It was a moment for reflection; I absorbed the solitude, the raw power of nature surrounding me, and I felt a profound connection to this remarkable place that had witnessed such chaos.

Shelly and I were on a mission, we'd have time to reflect once we got to camp for the night. We continued our journey. Each step we took brought us closer to our destination and deeper into the heart of Mount St. Helen's untamed wilderness. The adventure was far from over, and I couldn't wait to see what lay ahead.

As we made our way through the heart of the volcanic breach, the trail opened up onto a flat plateau, leading us across several more gullies. My leg started to spasm frequently at this point, which slowed our pace considerably. Shelly kept pace with me without a word of complaint, though her concern was clear in her expression. I wasn't entirely sure what was going on with my muscles; I just assumed it was due to overuse from the hike.

As the sun sank lower in the sky, we finally reached the plateau above the South Fork of the Toutle River. The views were absolutely breathtaking. The landscape was scattered with plants that reminded me of wild strawberry bushes, while the ground was softened by a carpet of moss and pumice. It felt like one of the most beautiful spots I had encountered along the trail thus far.

From where we stood, we had a stunning view of the Mount St. Helens Toutle and Talus glaciers, which were partially covered by a layer of ash. They rested on the mountain's face, overlooking the steep canyon of the Toutle River. I recalled reading that this river had taken the brunt of volcanic debris during the eruption, which had helped carve out the deep and wide canyon we were looking at. Standing on this plateau, it even felt like we were on a beach along the West Coast at times, with the rugged beauty surrounding us.

After taking in the breathtaking view, our next goal was to make it down the steep canyon wall before the sun set, so we could reach the bank of the Toutle River below. The trail leading into the canyon was covered entirely in ash and sand, which wasn't a surprise at this point. I navigated slowly and steadily over a series of partially washed-out switchbacks, carefully making my way down into the canyon.

From the top of the plateau to the Toutle valley, it was close to a 1,700-foot elevation loss over a very short distance. My legs were beginning to feel the effects of this waterless journey so far, each step reminding me of the effort it took to conquer the trail. The ash and sand underfoot shifted with every movement, making it challenging to find my footing as I descended. I had to concentrate, not only on my pace but also on the slip of the earth beneath me. Despite the fatigue setting in, the thrill of adventure spurred me on, as I could almost hear the call of the river below, promising respite and refreshment at the journey's end of day one. The final 40 feet of descent involved a steep drop off the edge of the canyon, landing us right on the riverbed. To help with climbing down and back up the loose soil and rocks, a rope was installed.

Once we arrived at the Toutle River, we were relieved to discover that the blast zone restrictions had been lifted, allowing us to camp there. The descent into the Toutle Canyon was breathtaking, and after a long day of hiking, I was happy to set up camp by the river for the night. I wanted to avoid the riverbed itself and suggested we find a spot on the south side of the riverbank. After climbing out of the riverbed, we found ourselves surrounded by a mix of new and old growth trees, with a soft layer of moss covering the pumice beneath our feet. I suggested we camp there for the night.

With no chance of rain, we decided to leave the tent behind when we placed this hike. Instead, we spread our bivy bags on a flat patch of moss-covered ash and sand and made ourselves comfortable. The soothing sound of flowing water calmed my mind, and I felt a wave of relief as I settled in to rest. We were ready for a well-deserved night of sleep, feeling accomplished and excited for the adventures that awaited us the next day. Shelly, concerned about my leg, suggested I rest as much as possible, and we agreed to see how I felt about the steep climb out of the valley in the morning.

I refilled my water, cooked dinner, and enjoyed the beautiful alpenglow on the mountain before darkness fell. As I lay in my bivy, the emotions of the day's journey began to wash over me. I was overcome with a deep sadness that my Dad wasn't able to join me on this hike. It felt like just yesterday that we had made plans to explore the Loowit Trail together, mapping out every detail with excitement and anticipation. I wanted him to be proud of me and longed for his presence on this adventure. The solitude of the canyon only amplified the absence I felt.

I whispered a silent promise to him, vowing to carry on our shared love for the wilderness and the mountains, even if he couldn't be there physically. This hike was as much for him as it was for me, a testament to our bond and the adventures we had dreamed of. With these thoughts, I found a sense of peace, knowing that, in spirit, he was with me every step of the way.

Once night arrived, I quickly drifted off to sleep, lulled by the twinkling stars above and the sound of the rushing river nearby.

BUTTE CAMP

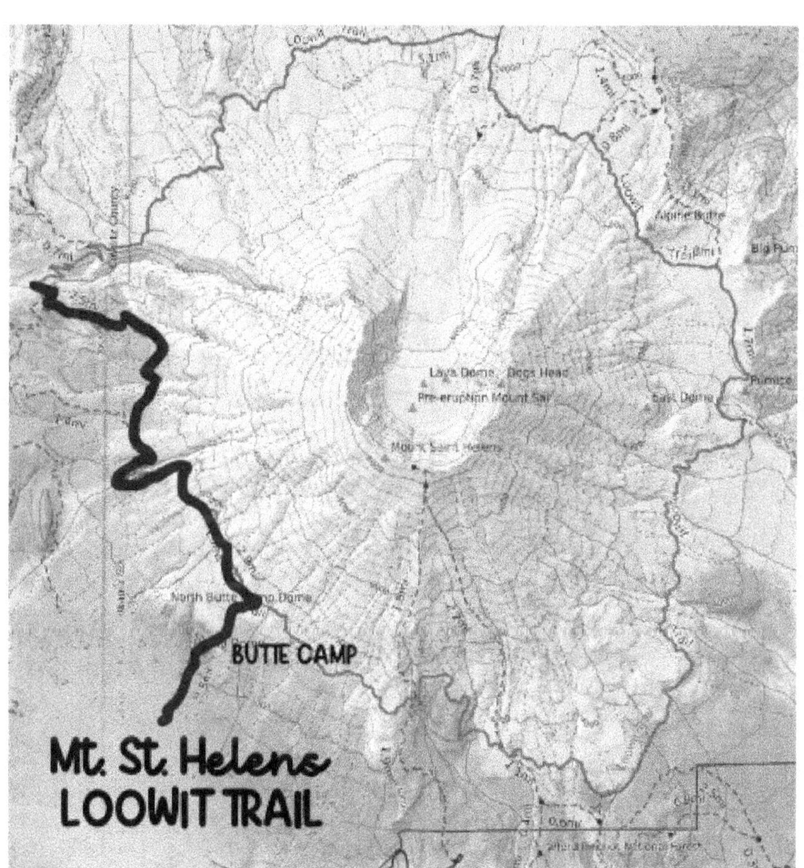

AS THE SUN ROSE ON the second day of our adventure, we were greeted by a refreshing chill in the air, accompanied by the calming sound of the Toutle River gently flowing nearby. I could sense that today would be a test of my endurance, but I was resolute in my decision to continue my journey counterclockwise on the 360-degree loop that would eventually lead me back to my car parked at Windy Ridge. The first order of business was to climb out of my bivy bag and pack up my gear once more. This thought felt somewhat daunting, especially considering the challenging miles of ascent that awaited me through a rare forested section of the trail.

As we began our hike, the path took us through dense woods, a striking contrast to the arid landscapes we had traversed just the day before. The thick canopy overhead provided a much-needed shield from the morning sun, casting playful dappled shadows on the trail beneath our feet. However, I couldn't ignore the strain in my leg, a reminder of the exertions from the previous day. Each step was a small battle, echoing the spasms and fatigue that had been my companions since we started this journey. I made an effort to push those negative thoughts aside, focusing instead on the rhythmic sound of my footsteps hitting the ground and the fresh, earthy scent of the forest that filled my lungs.

The trail continued to wind its way upward, revealing glimpses of the imposing Mount St. Helens as we ascended higher towards Crescent Ridge. Seeing the majestic volcano, partially obscured by the treetops, was both awe-inspiring and a little intimidating. My mind wavered between feelings of determination and moments of doubt. I was trying hard to cultivate a positive mindset, reminding myself of the ultimate goal and the sense of achievement that would await me at the end of this challenging journey. Yet, as I trudged up the steep incline, the struggle felt very real, and my optimism began to wane with each painful step I took.

Despite the physical challenges, I was determined to keep moving forward. Every ounce of effort seemed worth it as I envisioned the breathtaking views and the sense of accomplishment that awaited me at the end. I reminded myself that this was more than just a hike; it was an opportunity to push my limits and discover what I was truly capable of. With each step, I drew strength from the beauty surrounding me, hoping that the challenges I faced today would only make my eventual triumph even sweeter.

As we climbed closer to the top of the steep switchback ascent, a wave of exhaustion washed over me, leaving me feeling utterly drained. My legs were struggling to keep up with the demanding trail, and the intense electrical sensations shooting through my muscles were becoming increasingly unbearable. Each jolt of pain echoed like a cruel reminder of my limitations, and I realized I couldn't ignore it any longer.

I decided to stop, leaning heavily on a tree along the trail for support. I turned to Shelly, who had been hiking alongside me. "I'm really concerned about my leg," I admitted, my voice laced with frustration and worry. "It's getting worse, and the sensations are just too much to handle."

Shelly, always the compassionate listener, paused and gave me a reassuring nod. "Let's take a moment to rest and assess the situation," she suggested gently. Her calm demeanor acted as a soothing balm to my frazzled nerves, and I found a small measure of comfort just by having her there.

We found a nearby rock and settled down, allowing our surroundings to envelop us. The vast expanse of the landscape stretched out before us, a breathtaking sight that reminded me why I had embarked on this journey in the first place. As I sat there, taking deep breaths and trying to regain my strength, I couldn't help but wonder if I had the stamina to continue. The journey ahead seemed daunting, filled with uncertainty and challenges, but I knew I couldn't give up.

This hike was more than just a physical challenge; it was a test of my resolve and spirit. With every step I had taken, I had pushed myself to confront the limits of my endurance. In recognition of Shelly's unwavering support by my side, I felt a glimmer of hope that maybe, just maybe, I could push through the pain and complete this journey. The beauty of nature around us, combined with the determination bubbling within me, sparked a renewed sense of purpose. I resolved to keep moving forward, one careful step at a time.

Shelly's diagnosis was delivered with a confident smile that immediately put me at ease. "I'm certain you can walk it off," she said reassuringly. "Just be sure to stop and take some breaks along the way." Her words felt like a flicker of hope in my otherwise uncertain situation, and after a brief rest, we decided to continue our hike once more, determined to enjoy the day.

As we walked, we soon reached the split in the trail where Sheep Canyon veered off to the right. This particular spot brought a rush of memories flooding back to me. It was here that my Dad and I had hiked together on a previous trip, and the nostalgia hit me again like a wave. I couldn't help but reminisce about the plans we had made to explore the Loowit Trail, dreams that now felt bittersweet as I thought of those cherished moments.

Almost as if on cue, the familiar gullies reappeared along our path! Just like the day before, we came upon another steep gully, complete with ropes installed to help us navigate the challenging climb up and down the steep slope of ash and sand. This gully was particularly difficult, and I quickly realized I needed Shelly's expertise to help me get through it safely. To my surprise, I learned that she was an avid member of the CrossFit community, which explained her impressive strength and determination. Out of all the people I could have been hiking with, having Shelly by my side felt like a blessing I hadn't anticipated. Her support made me feel more confident, and together we tackled the challenges ahead, ready to take on whatever the trail had in store for us.

As we navigated around the southwest side of the mountain, I was once again taken aback by the changing landscape. The rugged terrain transformed into a relatively flat alpine tundra, providing a welcome relief and making the walking much easier for a time. The views surrounding me were nothing short of spectacular; Mount St. Helens loomed majestically above us, casting its imposing shadow, while layers of forested hills stretched out along the horizon, including the iconic Mt. Hood further to the south. It was a serene and breathtaking sight, one that temporarily helped to distract me from the pain that was coursing through my legs after hours of hiking.

However, despite the more manageable terrain, the electric sensations in my legs only seemed to grow stronger, and I could feel the strain beginning to take a toll on my hip as well. For the first time during our journey, I noticed that Shelly had moved quite ahead of me, creating an increasing distance between us with each step she took. I watched her figure shrink in the distance, feeling a mixture of frustration and determination building inside me. The pain was relentless, but deep down, I knew I had to keep pushing forward. This hike was not just about reaching a destination; it was a true test of my resolve and endurance, and I wasn't ready to throw in the towel just yet. I could feel the weight of the challenge ahead, but I was determined to rise to it, step by step.

The Loowit Trail, which had been an exhilarating journey so far, took an unexpected turn after what felt like about a mile. It suddenly came to an abrupt halt at the gaping washout of Coldspring Canyon. My heart raced for a moment! However, there was no need to panic once I looked around, as a new detour had been constructed to help guide us around this obstacle. Shelly, my trusty hiking companion, had paused to wait for me to catch up, ready to tackle the gigantic detour that lay ahead of us.

We began our journey down the detour, which led us 400 feet along the edge of the canyon. The rocky terrain was both beautiful and intimidating, with the sheer drop below reminding us of the thrill and danger of the mountain. As we made our way, we soon came across a fixed rope that stretched down into a narrow slot leading to the canyon floor. This rope was not just a helpful tool; it was nearly essential for what we affectionately called "batmanning" down a steep 10-foot vertical bank at the bottom. The descent required careful maneuvering, and I felt a mix of excitement and apprehension.

This moment was the true test of our hiking skills and endurance. I couldn't help but wonder how much more of this adventure I could handle. Ahead of us, the south side of the mountain loomed with gullies and boulders scattered throughout the landscape—could I master this rugged terrain? After taking a deep breath, I used another fixed rope to pull myself up the opposite bank, where we hiked along the canyon, determined to regain the 400 feet we lost in our detour.

As soon as we returned to the original Loowit Trail, we picked up our pace, a sense of urgency creeping in as we thought about our timing. I could see the concern etched on Shelly's face; we both knew we had to get to the car before nightfall. With the sun making progress in the horizon, we pushed ourselves forward, motivated by the thought of completing our trek and the adventure we had shared. Would we make it back in time?

As we approached a turnoff for a feeder trail leading to Butte Camp, we decided it was time to take a break and regroup. The air was thick with the silence that often precedes a serious conversation, and I knew it was time to be honest with Shelly. With a heavy heart and a voice weighed down by doubt and exhaustion, I opened up to her. "I'm massively concerned that I can't do the next section of the trail," I admitted, feeling the weight of my worries hanging over me like a dark cloud.

Shelly paused for a moment, looking at me thoughtfully. Her expression was a mix of concern and determination, and then she said, "I could trail run to the parking lot and drive the car back to the Butte Camp trailhead." Her suggestion was practical, but I could sense her determination behind it.

I thought she was completely insane. The idea of her running the trail alone while I waited in pain felt impossible and frightening. The thought of being left behind while she navigated the trail without me was daunting. Yet, as I stood there, contemplating my next move, my mind drifted back to my Dad. Memories of him flooded my thoughts—his unwavering support and encouragement when I faced challenges on the trail. What would he do in this situation? He would tell me to push through, to dig deep and find the strength within myself to keep going, no matter how tough it seemed.

With Shelly's support and the memory of my Dad's enduring spirit driving me forward, I realized I had to make a decision. This journey was about so much more than just reaching my car at the end of the trail; it was about proving to myself that I could overcome any obstacle in my path, just as my Dad would have wanted me to. The thought of letting doubt win was unbearable. With renewed resolve, I decided I wouldn't let fear hold me back.

I made the decision to accept Shelly's offer, feeling a rush of relief in making the decision. Without a moment of hesitation, she quickly merged her gear with mine, tossing everything into my pack, and took off with just a water bottle in her hand, trail running like a woman on a mission. It was impressive to watch her cover miles with such speed, her figure soon disappearing from view as she dashed ahead.

As I paused to regroup, I pulled out the map again to assess what lay ahead on the journey. The Butte Camp trail wasn't clearly marked regarding its exact length, but from what I could figure out, it seemed like it would be a couple of miles to reach the start of the trailhead at Red Rock Pass, where we had agreed to meet. I was determined to hike the decline at a slow and steady pace; after all, I was looking forward to resting for a while before Shelly arrived. Taking a deep breath to steady my nerves, I began my hike once again.

The view along the trail was nothing short of breathtaking, the stunning beauty of the landscape offering a welcome distraction from the rapid change of plans that had been thrust upon us. I found solace in the sights surrounding me, which made the hike feel less daunting. Although descending at this angle was challenging, it was definitely more manageable than navigating through gullies, washouts, or drastic elevation changes. The trail wound gracefully through lush meadows, revealing expansive vistas of the surrounding mountains at every turn.

With each step, I felt a bit more at ease as I focused on the incredible scenery, the fresh mountain air filling my lungs and renewing my spirit. Despite the persistent pain in my leg, I found a rhythm, moving steadily downhill. Thoughts of my Dad and the goal of reaching Red Rock Pass kept me motivated. This part of the trail, although demanding, served as a testament to the journey itself—a beautiful blend of struggle and beauty, pain and perseverance.

I finally reached Butte Camp, and I have to say, it took me by surprise. It was a very small and rustic campground, seemingly optimized for just two or three tents at most. There was no water source nearby, nor were there any breathtaking views to enjoy. Instead, it was tucked away in the thick of an old-growth forest, perched on what looked like another small volcano that surrounded the mighty Mt. St. Helens. As I paused for a brief moment to drink some bottled water and catch my breath, I felt a wave of exhaustion wash over me. I knew I had to get back on the trail, but that was when the enormity of the pain I was experiencing really started to hit me.

Frustration and desperation set in as I pulled out my phone, checking what it felt like every 30 seconds. I was determined to find at least one bar of service to make a call. At that moment, I had no clue who I might call for help, but I knew I needed assistance. After about fifteen minutes of distracted hiking, I finally saw the signal I had been hoping for—one bar on my phone! Without missing a beat, I dialed my best friend, Dave. I quickly explained the trail I was on and the tough situation I was facing. My anxiety started to grow as I worried that Shelly might take too long to find me, especially given that it was easily a two hour drive from the parking lot to the trailhead.

Dave listened attentively, taking notes and reassuring me with his calm voice. "Just go to the trailhead and stay put," he advised confidently. "I'll see you as soon as I can get there." Trying not to let the weight of defeat crush me, I packed up my gear again and began the slow walk down the trail. By this point, my leg was starting to drag, and I felt constant electrical shock sensations coursing through it. I wasn't exactly sure what was going on with my body, but I was resolute in my determination to reach the trailhead.

As I trudged along, I had no idea that I still had about two more miles to go. The journey was slow, and my mind was a whirlwind of thoughts racing in every direction. I caught sight of a chipmunk darting along the trail, its tiny feet pattering lightly on the ground. For just a moment, the simplicity of its movements provided a brief distraction from the pain and uncertainty that hung over me like a dark cloud. Each step felt like a battle, but I knew I had to keep moving forward. One foot in front of the other, I pushed through the discomfort, telling myself that I would reach my destination soon. Every ounce of determination I had surged through me as I continued down the trail, hoping for relief and a way out of this challenging situation.

I finally reached the bottom of the mountain, and what lay before me was nothing short of breathtaking. A vast lava field stretched out, dotted with larger-than-life boulders that seemed to go on forever, as far as my eyes could see. To my relief, the maintained trail wound right through this rocky terrain, sparing me the exhausting ordeal of boulder hopping. As I walked, I noticed that the path was surprisingly level, and with each step, I could sense that I was getting closer to the end of my long journey.

The lava field eventually came to an end at Red Rock Pass, which was the meeting point I had arranged with both Shelly and Dave. After what felt like an eternity—about two hours since I had said goodbye to Shelly—I finally spotted the trailhead sign that confirmed I had made it! Now, all that was left for me to do was wait for my rescue, a thought that filled me with both relief and anticipation.

Feeling utterly exhausted from the trek, I decided to unpack my entire bag. I took a long drink of water, munched on some food, and rolled out my bivy sack, curling up inside it to rest. It must have been a strange sight to see someone like me sprawled out in the middle of a trailhead parking lot, but at that moment, I was too tired to care. My mind was racing with thoughts about how long I might have to wait for my friends and whether they would be able to find me out here in the wilderness.

After lying down for only fifteen minutes, I suddenly heard the sound of a car approaching on the forest road. My heart raced as I turned to see who it was, and then around the corner came Dave. I was absolutely blown away by his arrival. It seemed like he must have left Vancouver the instant I had called him for help. In my pain and exhaustion, I had completely lost track of time; it felt like only moments had passed since our conversation. Overwhelmed with joy, I was left speechless, too drained even to shed a tear. You know you're in a special place when emotions hit you like that.

Dave quickly helped me pack up my gear while I recounted the details of my latest adventure. What a true friend he was! It's always a good idea to surround yourself with people who offer support and wise counsel—it really does take a village. He provided some much-needed encouragement and shared a broader perspective on what I had accomplished on this trek. Although Dave is a man of few words, when he did speak, his words carried a weight that resonated with me. I felt grateful to have him by my side.

Once we hopped into the car, we began the journey to the Windy Ridge trailhead, hoping to arrive there before Shelly. The adventure wasn't over yet, and I could feel the excitement bubbling within me. But with friends like Dave and Shelly, I knew I was in good hands, ready for whatever came next on this incredible journey.

As we headed towards Windy Ridge in Dave's car, I found myself reflecting on the short adventure I had embarked upon. My thoughts were all over the place, but I relished in the comfort of sitting down. Every time we passed a car going in the opposite direction, we slowed down to see if it was Shelly.

After about an hour, we were roughly halfway there when another car approached from the opposite direction. My heart leaped with joy—it was my car! Inside was Shelly, grinning ear to ear, super excited to see us. We waved her down and turned around to reconnect.

Shelly had managed to run the last fifteen plus miles to the car in the time it took me to hike just a few miles downhill to the trailhead. What a journey! And did I forget to mention that she did this whole adventure with a cast on one arm? Yep, that was Shelly.

Reunited, we shared stories and laughter, the trials of the trail already fading into the background. The journey had pushed us to our limits, but it also revealed our resilience and the strength of our friendships. With Dave and Shelly by my side, I felt ready for whatever the next adventure might bring. Confident that the chapter was closed for the Loowit Trail, I was content in all that I had accomplished. No, I hadn't done the entire trail in one attempt, but I was okay with all that I had learned along the way. If I do the trail again, I look forward to the unscripted adventures and challenges I will face.

MARATHON

AS I REFLECT ON MY journey through the Loowit Trail and life with Multiple Sclerosis, one thing stands out above all: resilience. The path wasn't always straight or easy, with its rugged landscapes and challenging terrains, but every twist and turn taught me something invaluable. Resilience is about finding the strength to keep going, even when the odds seem stacked against you. It's about getting back up, time and again, despite the challenges that threaten to hold you down.

Throughout my hikes, I learned that perseverance is the partner of resilience. It's the steady, determined push forward, the refusal to give up even when your body and spirit feel worn out. There were days when the trail seemed endless, with the sun beating down and the pumice burning, when each step felt heavier than the last. Yet, in those moments, I discovered a depth of strength I didn't know I had. It wasn't always about finishing the trail around my mountain; sometimes, it was simply about taking the next step, feeling the ground beneath my feet, and moving forward one foot at a time.

Multiple Sclerosis introduced me to obstacles I never anticipated. The disease taught me to adapt, to find new ways of doing old things, whether it meant adjusting how I packed my backpack or pacing myself differently on steep ascents, and to appreciate the small victories along the way—like reaching a new milestone or managing a particularly steep incline without needing to pause. Each time I set foot on a trail, I was reminded of the power of persistence. The journey wasn't just physical; it was a mental and emotional battle, too, testing my resolve and encouraging me to dig deep into reserves of courage I hadn't tapped before.

From my experiences, I realized that embracing challenges head-on is essential. On this epic mountain trail with its unpredictable paths and breathtaking beauty, it mirrored the unpredictability of life with adversity. Each hike taught me to prepare for the unexpected, bringing extra gear for unforeseen conditions, and to welcome the unknown as part of the adventure. I learned to rely on my faith, knowing that every setback was just a setup for a greater comeback.

These lessons became the foundation of my approach to life. In moments of doubt or when my body faltered due to the fatigue and symptoms of MS, I leaned on the strength I had built through my experiences. I learned that resilience isn't about never feeling afraid or overwhelmed; it's about facing those feelings with courage and resolve, rallying with every ounce of spirit. It's about finding joy in the journey, regardless of the obstacles along the way, cherishing each moment for what it teaches you.

The support of my community, friends and family alike, played a crucial role in my perseverance. Their stories of triumph and determination, along with their constant encouragement, reminded me that I wasn't alone, that others had faced and overcome their own challenges. Together, we created a network of strength that fueled our collective resilience, sharing tips, advice, and motivation, lifting each other up when the path seemed toughest.

My journey around the mountain and living with MS has been about more than just physical endurance. It has been a testament to the unyielding spirit within us all. It has shown me that resilience and perseverance can turn any challenge into an opportunity for growth, allowing us to emerge stronger and more determined. As I continue to navigate life's trails, I carry these lessons with me, ready to face whatever lies beyond the treeline, confident in the knowledge that I have the strength and support to conquer any obstacle.

Embarking on the Loowit Trail was more than just a hike; it was a journey filled with unexpected challenges and invaluable lessons. Each section of the trail was unique, offering its own set of hurdles that forced me to adapt and learn quickly. The trail taught me the significance of preparation, both for outdoor adventures and for life itself.

One of the first lessons I learned was about the scarcity of water. On certain stretches of the trail, water sources were few and far between. This lack of water taught me the importance of planning ahead and carrying enough supplies. It was a harsh reminder that in life, too, we must anticipate our needs and be ready for unexpected shortages.

Whether it's resources, time, or energy, being prepared can help us manage and overcome scarcity.

Another challenge was the burning pumice under the sun. The dust like pumice not only scorched my skin but also tested my resolve. I learned to protect myself by wearing long sleeves and pants, transforming discomfort into a lesson in shielding oneself from harsh conditions. This experience mirrored life's trials, where we often face uncomfortable situations but can find ways to protect ourselves and endure with the right precautions.

The trail itself was unstable, constantly shifting and unpredictable. Loose rocks, soft ground, and steep inclines demanded my full attention and adaptability. This instability taught me to remain flexible and alert, embracing change rather than resisting it. Life is much like this ever-changing path, full of surprises that require us to adjust our plans and strategies to keep moving forward.

These experiences on the Loowit made me more knowledgeable and better prepared for future hikes and life's challenges. Each lesson was a building block, strengthening my ability to face difficulties head-on. Preparation, I realized, is not just about packing the right gear or having a plan; it's about cultivating a mindset that welcomes learning from every twist and turn.

In life, just as on the trail, preparation helps us overcome obstacles with resilience and confidence. It empowers us to tackle problems with a proactive attitude, turning potential setbacks into opportunities for growth. By embracing preparation, we can navigate life's paths more smoothly, equipped to handle whatever comes our way.

This adventure was deeply intertwined with the presence of my Dad, whose approach to life has significantly shaped my own. His recent passing has left a profound void, and this book is dedicated to his memory and the lessons he imparted.

My father was a man of wisdom and quiet strength. He approached life with a calm determination, always finding joy in simple pleasures and valuing the people around him. His philosophy was one of resilience and kindness, constantly reminding me to cherish each moment and build strong connections with those I love. These values have become the foundation of my own outlook on life.

Our journey on the Loowit Trail began together, a testament to the bond we shared. As we hiked, his patience and guidance taught me to appreciate the beauty in every step. His support was unwavering, and his presence made even the most challenging parts of the trail feel less daunting. It's a journey I wish I could have repeated with him, savoring each hike and each shared story. The time I had with him was precious, but like many, I find myself wishing for more.

With friends by my side, I continued the journey on the trail, as my college years didn't allow hiking with my Dad around this trail as much as I would have hoped for. This experience underscored the value of having both family and friends. Like my father, my friends provided encouragement and support, helping me along the way. Their companionship was a source of strength, and together we shared the journey, honoring my father's influence.

The experience taught me that life's journey is enriched by the people we share it with. While the loss of my father is deeply felt, the support of my friends has been a comforting reminder that I am not alone. Both family and friends play crucial roles in our lives, offering love, support, and a sense of belonging. They help us grow, face challenges, and celebrate victories.

Reflecting on these relationships, I am filled with gratitude for the moments shared with my father and the continued support of my friends. His memory lives on in the lessons he taught me and in the strength I find in those around me. Though he is deeply missed, his influence remains a part of who I am and every step I take.

Mt. St. Helens ruggedness teaches important lessons in adaptability and resilience. As I walked its winding paths, surrounded by beautiful landscapes, I faced challenges that tested my limits. The unpredictably rough terrain required resourcefulness and courage. These experiences changed my journey and taught me how to handle life's unpredictability with an open heart and mind. The lessons learned help me face daily challenges, reminding me of the strength in embracing uncertainty.

One of the most unforgettable surprises was the changing trail. Each section brought a new challenge, turning into something different that required us to adapt. At first, this unpredictability was annoying because I never knew what would happen. However, I eventually learned to welcome these changes and embrace the unexpected. It reminded me of nature's power and beauty, showing its lively character. This journey taught me to appreciate the unexpected and find excitement in things that seemed difficult at first. Initially, these obstacles seemed daunting, but they taught me to be flexible and resourceful. I learned to adapt my route, finding my way section of trail at a time. This adaptability became a source of strength, showing me that change doesn't have to be feared but can lead to new and rewarding experiences.

For example, I faced in one season the sudden inability to perform everyday tasks, I was forced to adapt in ways I never imagined. Writing with my non-dominant hand became a daily exercise in patience and persistence, each journal entry marking a small victory as chicken-scratch evolved into legible words. Strengthening my legs required a profound commitment, demanding that I push through frustration and fatigue to regain mobility. The unwavering support of my family and the lessons from previous experiences fortified my resolve. They taught me that fighting through adversity wasn't an option; it was a necessity. These trials reinforced the importance of perseverance, reminding me that life's obstacles can sometimes lead to the most profound transformations. This season in particular contributed to my experience on the trail.

Life is filled with surprises. Embracing the unexpected has taught me to see change not as a disruption but as an opportunity for growth. By being open to new experiences and willing to adjust course, I discovered a resilience within myself that I hadn't known before. This mindset has helped me face life's uncertainties with confidence and grace.

The Loowit became more than just a physical challenge; it was a way for me to reclaim my life and prove to myself that I could achieve great things despite my condition. The experience taught me valuable lessons about resilience, determination, and the importance of setting goals. I was excited to see what I could accomplish as I continued forward, embracing the ups and downs along the way. Through this journey, I've learned that life's greatest adventures often begin with a step into the unknown.

Throughout my journey, my faith has been a steadfast companion and a source of immense strength. My walk with Jesus has been a guiding light, constantly reminding me of the power and comfort He brings. The verse from Nehemiah 8:10, "the joy of the Lord is your strength," resonates deeply with me, encapsulating my journey and the foundation upon which I have built my life.

Faith has played a crucial role in every challenge and triumph I have encountered. It has been the anchor that holds me steady, even when the seas of life are tumultuous. With Jesus by my side, I have managed to achieve feats that once seemed impossible. Among these accomplishments are completing two half marathons and a demanding 130-mile bike ride. Each mile was a testament to the strength and resilience that faith instills in me, pushing me forward even when my body felt weary.

These achievements were not just physical milestones; they were spiritual victories, each step fueled by the unwavering belief that I am never alone. My faith provided the courage to start these journeys and the endurance to finish them. The joy of the Lord truly became my strength, uplifting me during moments of doubt and fatigue.

In the midst of these endeavors, my focus has never wavered. It remains central to who I am and what I aspire to be. Jesus is more than a source of motivation; He is the core of my existence, influencing every decision and action. He has taught me to approach life with gratitude, to find strength in joy, and to face each day with renewed hope. Through Him I can and do accomplish all things, though they may not look like how I originally forecasted and planned, they wind up being way more fulfilling and filled with a legacy that lasts.

Reflecting on my journey, I am profoundly grateful for the presence of faith in my life. It has been a constant source of guidance and support, reminding me that with Jesus, all things are possible. My walk with Him continues to inspire and empower me, encouraging me to embrace life's challenges with confidence and grace. As I move forward, I carry this faith in my heart, knowing He will always be my greatest strength and source of joy.

When I first decided to hike this grand adventure, my expectations were pretty simple. I thought I could finish the whole trip in just one or maybe two outings. I assumed it would be an easy and straightforward adventure. The idea of completing the trail filled me with excitement. However, as life often does, things didn't go exactly as planned. What I thought would be a quick and easy trek turned into several smaller adventures, each with its own challenges and lessons. This change in my journey was more meaningful than I could have imagined. It led me to discover a lot about myself and revealed a strength inside me that I didn't know I had.

As I started walking on the trail, I quickly realized that my original plan was too ambitious and a bit naive. The Loowit Trail is more rugged and challenging than I had anticipated. It demanded far more time, patience, and preparation than I initially expected. Due to this new reality, I had to change my approach. I began to break the trail into smaller sections that were easier to manage. This change wasn't just about logistics; it became a metaphor for how I deal with the various challenges that life throws at me.

Through these smaller journeys, I learned a lot about myself. Each mini adventure taught me something new about what I can do and where my limits are. There were times when I really had to push myself through tough parts of the trail, and in doing so, I discovered a strength and determination within me. On the other hand, I also faced moments of weakness where I felt tired and filled with self doubt. These moments were important too because they made me confront my vulnerabilities and showed me where I needed to improve.

This process of self discovery was very impactful and transformative. It taught me how I react when I'm under pressure, how I adapt to changes, and how I keep going even when things get hard. The trail acted like a mirror, showing me both my strengths and weaknesses. It gave me valuable insights into my character and resilience. I realized that my journey was more than just a physical challenge; it was also a mental exploration of who I am.

The whole experience was life-changing. It showed me that personal growth often comes from unexpected detours and challenges. I learned to embrace these experiences, understanding that each step—whether easy or difficult—was helping me grow. The Loowit was no longer just a path to be conquered; it became a journey of self discovery and inner strength. This journey left a lasting impact on my life and changed how I see myself. What started as a simple hike turned into a deep exploration of who I am, teaching me that sometimes, the journey itself is the true destination.

As I think back on my journey, one clear theme shines through everything: gratitude. This entire experience, with its ups and downs, has deeply influenced how I see my life. It has taught me to value each moment and every lesson that comes my way.

Every single step, whether it was easy or tough, contributed to a better understanding of myself and the world around me. The obstacles I encountered, from unexpected health issues to the rough terrain of the trail, were not just barriers to overcome. They were opportunities for me to learn and grow. These experiences helped me develop a sense of gratitude for discovering my own resilience and strength.

Gratitude has changed the way I look at the world. It has taught me to appreciate the small victories and the lessons hidden within setbacks. Each moment on the trail, whether it was the breathtaking views or the quiet times of reflection, filled me with appreciation for the beauty and unpredictability of life. This mindset has helped me embrace both the highs and lows, understanding that each has its purpose in my journey.

The lessons I learned on the trail have stretched beyond just the physical experience, influencing my outlook on life as a whole.

Gratitude has become a guiding principle in my life. It encourages me to see life with a renewed sense of purpose and understanding. I am reminded to be thankful for the support of friends and family, the strength of my faith, and the personal growth that comes from facing life's challenges head-on.

As I was growing up, my Dad was the one who guided and inspired me in the world of outdoor adventures. His love for nature was more than just a hobby; it was a way of life that was incredibly contagious. I am extremely grateful for his influence on me. He encouraged me to have a deep and lasting respect for the natural world. Whether it was camping trips, early morning hikes, or simply observing the changing seasons, his enthusiasm planted in me a passion that has been central to my life. I'm thankful his love for the outdoors rubbed off on me, as it has enriched my life in countless ways. It constantly reminds me of the joy and peace found in nature's embrace.

In every step I take, both on and off the trail, I carry this sense of gratitude with me. It has enhanced my life, providing a foundation of positivity and resilience. By focusing on gratitude, I have gained a wider perspective, one that values the journey just as much as the destination. This perspective has empowered me to face the future with confidence, knowing that each experience, whether planned or unexpected, is an opportunity to learn, grow, and be thankful.

As this journey comes to a close, I find myself reflecting on the myriad of experiences that have shaped my life. Each chapter in this book has been a testament to the strength and resilience that emerged from confronting my health challenges head-on. From the unpredictable trials of the Loowit Trail to the unwavering support of my faith, every moment has been a part of a greater story, woven with determination, hope, and the incredible power of the human spirit.

Nature's beauty has been both a sanctuary and a source of inspiration. The majestic landscapes and serene trails have not only tested my physical limits but have also offered solace and clarity. Through every twist and turn, the trails have mirrored the unpredictable journey of life, teaching me to embrace the unexpected and to find joy in the present moment.

Central to my journey has been the deepening relationship with my Heavenly Father. In moments of doubt and struggle, His love was a guiding light, illuminating the path forward. This bond has been unbreakable, providing strength when my own seemed depleted. My faith has been a cornerstone, reminding me that I am never alone and that His love and support can transform even the darkest moments.

As you turn the final page of this book, I hope you carry with you the message of hope and perseverance. Life's challenges may seem overwhelming at times, but they are also opportunities for profound transformation. Embrace your journey, no matter how daunting it may appear. Trust in His strength, lean on Him, and cherish the support of those around you.

May this story inspire you to rise above your own obstacles and to see each challenge as a stepping stone toward a life of fulfillment and purpose. Remember that there is no limit to what you can achieve, your limit is beyond the treeline.

FIRST CHAPTER OF THE NATIONAL PARK CONSPIRACY

THE ENTRANCE TO BITTERCREEK National Park loomed ahead, its wrought iron archway cloaked in ivy and moss, as though nature itself sought to reclaim it. The faded lettering, warped and barely legible after decades of exposure to the elements, bore the park's name, with rusty streaks marking its surface like old scars. The gate creaked faintly in the breeze, an unsteady sound that seemed out of place in the stillness. Beyond it, towering pine trees stretched skyward, their jagged forms interlocking to create a canopy that dappled the ground below with fragmented light. The shadows they cast seemed alive, rippling despite the absence of wind, as if the trees were whispering secrets to one another. A weathered handmade signpost stood at the entrance, leaning slightly to one side with the warning: "*Caution: Enter at Your Own Risk.*" Beneath the handmade sign, an official park sign featuring smaller lettering informed visitors about the park's rugged terrain and remote nature, though it failed to mention the unspoken truth—about the disappearances and the unease that clung to the place like a second skin.

Dan Harper adjusted the straps of his weathered backpack, the leather cracked and frayed from years of use. His fingers lingered on the fabric, a subconscious gesture of reassurance, as he glanced toward the others in his group. His face, lined with age, compassion, and a quiet sorrow he rarely spoke of, softened as his eyes swept over them. Leading this trip hadn't been an easy decision. It was supposed to be a chance for connection and reflection, but the park's reputation hung over him like a storm cloud. He had tried to reassure them on the drive up, his voice steady as he said, "God's creation. Even the wildest places can be redeemed." Yet as he stood at the edge of the darkened trailhead, staring into the dense forest ahead, he couldn't shake the gnawing unease in his gut. There was more to this place than untamed beauty. He could feel it in the air, heavy and oppressive.

Sarah Bennett wiped her brow and shifted uncomfortably in her hiking boots, breaking Dan's train of thought. The single mother had never been much of an outdoors enthusiast. She preferred the buzz of city life, where the chaos at least felt familiar. But her son Ryan had always loved hiking, his eyes lighting up at the idea of exploring trails and climbing rocks. This trip was supposed to be her way of bridging the gap between them, of showing him she could step into his world just as much as he stepped into hers. She clutched his photo in her jacket pocket, her fingers tracing its edges as a soft grimace tugged at her lips. The thought of him kept her going, but now, as she stood at the forest's edge, the towering trees casting ominous shadows over their group, a pit of doubt settled in her stomach. "This doesn't feel right," she muttered under her breath, her voice barely audible.

"What doesn't feel right?" Jack "J.D." Dawson's gravelly voice cut through her thoughts. He folded his arms across his chest, the ink of his military tattoo peeking out from beneath his rolled up sleeve. His broad shoulders and rugged demeanor gave him an air of confidence, but his sharp eyes scanned their surroundings with a wariness borne of years in the field. J.D. wasn't a man who scared easily (he had seen his share of danger) but he also believed in trusting his instincts. And right now, his instincts were on high alert. Something about this place set him on edge, though he wasn't about to admit it outright.

Sarah glanced at him, hesitating before replying. "Just... I don't know. It's the stillness," she said quietly, her eyes flicking toward the forest edge. "Everything here feels... wrong."

J.D. snorted lightly, though there was no real humor in it. Adjusting the brim of his beat up cap, he said, "That's just nature, city gal. Quiet's what you're supposed to hear out here." His voice carried a faint edge of impatience, but his posture didn't relax.

From the back of the group, a small voice chimed in, breaking the brief silence. "Sometimes quiet isn't peaceful," Lily Martinez said, her tone soft but matter-of-fact. At twelve years old, she was the youngest of their group, her petite form almost swallowed by her oversized jacket and the tiny backpack slung across her shoulders. Her dark eyes were thoughtful, too old for her years, and there was a quiet strength about her that belied her age. The group had found her weeks ago visiting the church one Sunday, shy and silent. Dan had taken her in, sensing an unspoken pain in her silence, and she had followed them here without complaint. Now, she hugged herself tightly, shuffling closer to Dan as though seeking reassurance. Despite her age, she seemed unimpressed by J.D.'s bravado and unimpressed still by Sarah's unease. She simply stared at the forest, her gaze steady.

Dan knelt beside her, his voice warm and steady as he said, "You'll be okay with all of us, you know." His words seemed to settle something in her, and she gave him a small, hesitant nod. The quiet faith she placed in him was evident, and it anchored him as much as he hoped it anchored her.

The group stood at the trailhead for a moment longer, the air thick with unspoken tension. The forest loomed ahead, its darkened depths inviting yet foreboding, as though daring them to step inside. Finally, with a deep breath, Dan straightened and gestured for the group to move forward. "Let's stick together," he said, his voice firm yet reassuring. The words hung in the air as they took their first steps onto the path, the shadows swallowing them whole. Behind them, the rusty gate stood silent, its warning long since faded into the overgrowth.

Dr. Emily Carter wrinkled her nose as she unfolded the map, the brittle paper crackling slightly in her hands. "I'm surprised any trails here are still usable. Frankly, there isn't enough maintenance data on this area for comfort, and that makes me uneasy." Her voice was brisk, clipped, but her movements were precise and deliberate, like someone accustomed to carrying the weight of her thoughts. Emily was the type of person who never stopped calculating, never stopped analyzing, her mind a constant hum of hypotheses and variables. It showed in her demeanor, in the way she clutched the map just a little too tightly. Her childhood faith, once warm and unshakable, had corroded over time, tarnished by unanswered prayers and the cold, sharp edges of science. She glanced around at the looming trees, her expression unreadable. "You'd think multiple disappearances would prompt some kind of investigation, wouldn't you?"

J.D. snorted, his lips twisting in a bitter smirk as he hooked his hands into his belt loops. "Government doesn't investigate unless it makes 'em money or headlines," he said, shaking his head. "Neither apply here.

This place ain't exactly a tourist trap, and God knows local officials don't care about a couple of missing hikers." His tone was flippant, but there was a defensive edge to it, like he was trying to mask his own unease beneath a layer of cynicism.

Dan, who had been crouched by his bag checking supplies, rose slowly, his calm, steady presence a stark contrast to J.D.'s sharpness. His eyes flickered between his companions, his gaze soft yet resolute. "We're not here for conspiracy theories," he said firmly but kindly, his voice carrying a quiet authority that invited trust. "We're here to enjoy what the Lord made and see what He has in store for us all. Stay together, respect the trail, and we'll be fine. God doesn't lead us anywhere without a purpose."

"Respect the trail," J.D. muttered under his breath, rolling his eyes. "What are we, kids on a field trip?" Despite his sarcasm, his hand lingered near the knife strapped to his belt, fingers brushing the worn leather handle. His slouched posture straightened ever so slightly as he moved forward, his expression hardening like someone preparing for an unseen challenge.

The group had first come together at the church Dan led, united by their shared love for the outdoors and a thirst for adventure. Nestled in their small town, the church had become more than a place of worship. It was a hub for like minded individuals seeking camaraderie beyond Sunday services. Dan had organized countless hiking trips, camping excursions, and even a few survival workshops, fostering a tight knit community bound by trust and resilience. Over time, these shared experiences in the wild forged bonds that went deeper than words, creating a group that felt more like family than friends.

Their latest adventure led them to Bittercreek National Park, a hidden gem chosen for its untouched beauty and rugged trails. Known for its towering thick pine forests, the park offered a sense of tranquility and solitude that was hard to find elsewhere. The group was eager to explore this little used area of the state, drawn to the promise of uncovering hidden vistas, secluded clearings, and the sounds of nature uninterrupted by human activity. It was the perfect setting for their next chapter of discovery and connection.

The group fell into an unsteady formation, Dan taking the lead with Emily close by his side, her map still unfurled and her eyes darting between the faded contours on the paper and the shadowed landscape ahead. Behind them, Sarah and Lily kept to the center, staying close together like nervous birds, their heads swiveling toward every faint rustle or whisper in the brush. J.D. brought up the rear, his booted steps slow and deliberate, his head on a constant swivel as he scanned the forest with the wary air of a hunter entering unfamiliar territory. The weight of the silence pressed down on them, broken only by the crunch of their footsteps and the occasional snap of a twig.

The deeper they ventured into Bittercreek, the darker their path became. Towering trees loomed overhead, their gnarled branches knitting together to form an almost impenetrable canopy that blotted out the sun. The forest floor was dappled with shifting patches of murky light, and the air grew noticeably cooler as they ascended. The earthy scent of pine filled their lungs, mingling with the faint, sour tang of decay that lingered just beneath the surface, like something the forest was trying to hide.

Their path narrowed as they came to a stop at a weathered wooden marker where the trail split off in several directions. The signpost was ancient, its wood splintered and grayed with age, the carved lettering so worn it was nearly unreadable. Dan stepped forward, his brow furrowed as he reached out to brush away the moss clinging to the post. His fingers were inches from the rough surface when Emily's sharp voice broke the silence.

"Wait," she said, her tone urgent as she grabbed his arm. Her eyes were fixed on the weathered wood, her expression tightening as she pointed. "Look."

The moss wasn't alone in climbing the post. Beneath its green tendrils, something else caught the faint light filtering through the trees. A crude etching, thin and jagged, had been scratched into the wood as though by someone in a desperate hurry. It was an arrow, pointing off to one of the trails, and beneath it, faint but unmistakable, was a single word.

Help.

For a moment, no one spoke. The forest seemed to hold its breath, the stillness pressing in around them like a living thing.

"Well, that's cheerful," J.D. said finally, his voice dark and low. His hand drifted back to his belt, fingers grazing the hilt of his knife as his eyes narrowed on the ominous etching. Everyone stood frozen, the weight of the word sinking into their minds like a stone dropped into deep water.

Dan stared at the etching, his eyes tracing each jagged groove, until his pulse pressed hard against his throat. The word seemed to claw at his mind, demanding attention. "It's just graffiti," he said quietly but unconvincingly, his voice barely above a whisper as though speaking too loudly might awaken something.

"Graffiti way out here?" Sarah asked, her face pale, her lips pressed into a thin line. Her arms crossed tightly over her chest as if shielding herself. "What kind of prank is that? Who even comes this far just to do something like this?"

"Don't overthink it." Emily's voice cut in, sharper than she intended. She glanced at Lily, who was shifting her feet nervously, her hands clutching the straps of her backpack like a lifeline. "We don't need to scare ourselves over something that's probably been here for years." Her tone was steady, but her eyes betrayed her doubt. Even her scientific certainty, usually unshakeable, wavered. She studied the etching again, her brow furrowed, but quickly turned away as though looking too long might give it power.

Dan nodded curtly, more to himself than anyone else, and gestured for the group to follow. "Let's just keep moving," he muttered, and led them to the right, down the arrowed trail. The air seemed to thicken with every step, as though the forest itself was closing in. Their breaths grew shallow, the usual tranquility of the woods replaced by something far heavier, more ominous. The silence was broken only by the rhythmic crunch of boots on fallen leaves and the occasional birdsong, but even these sounds felt muted, distant.

Yet amidst the normal hum of the forest, there was something else. Something faint, almost imperceptible. A low, steady vibration, like a hum just beyond the threshold of human hearing. It was the kind of sound you almost didn't notice at first, but once you did, it became impossible to ignore. It seemed to emanate from all around them, seeping into their bones.

J.D., who had been at the front of the group, stopped abruptly. His hand shot up in a silent signal, fingers stiff with tension. The group froze behind him, their hearts pounding in unison, the tension palpable.

"What is it?" Emily whispered, her voice barely audible. She gripped the strap of her bag tightly, her knuckles whitening.

J.D. tilted his head, listening intently. His gaze darted between the trees, scanning the dense woods for answers. "Not sure," he murmured, his voice low and cautious. "Just... stay close." His words carried a weight that made the others exchange nervous glances, their confidence in him wavering for the first time.

With that, they pressed on, the trail spiraling deeper into the forest's clutch. The canopy overhead grew denser, casting long, stretched shadows across the path. The shadows seemed to slither and shift, like barriers torn from something obscene and unseen. Behind them, the signpost remained, its desperate word etched so deeply into the wood it seemed as though it had been carved with desperation itself. Help.

No one spoke much after that. Words felt unnecessary—worse, they felt dangerous, as though the forest might punish their intrusion by swallowing their voices altogether. The air seemed to press down on them, thick and oppressive, making every breath a little harder. Even the birds had grown silent, their absence amplifying the faint hum that continued to grow in their ears.

Dan glanced over his shoulder, his nerves on edge. He couldn't shake the unsettling sensation of being watched. This was supposed to be a simple group hike through the local National Park, a chance to enjoy nature together. Sure, the park had a dark reputation for its history of mysterious disappearances, but they had assumed safety came in numbers when planning the trip. Now, every step felt heavier, as if unseen eyes were tracking their every move. He noticed Sarah glancing around as well, her hand twitching anxiously at her side as they walked.

Ahead of them, the path narrowed, winding through a stretch of trees so close together they felt like sentinels. The light barely reached the ground here, and the earthy smell of damp moss and rotting leaves grew stronger. It was as though the forest itself was alive, breathing, watching. The oppressive stillness pressed against their ears, and though there were no cries for help on the trail, the forest, in its ancient and unyielding silence, seemed to whisper all the same.

It whispered of things forgotten, things that didn't belong to the world outside. And though none of them would admit it, each member of the group could feel it. A growing certainty that they were walking into something they couldn't explain, and perhaps wouldn't escape.

TO BE CONTINUED...

Continue reading The National Park Conspiracy by scanning the QR Code below.

Did you enjoy reading this book from Ryan Thompson?

You can find more books from him by scanning the QR Code below or visiting eppublishers.com.

Books by Ryan Thompson

Standalone:

Architects of Chaos

Beyond the Treeline

Catacomb Network

Ghosts of Langley

The National Park Conspiracy

Margaret Swanson Thrillers:

Packwood

Sandpoint

Bend

Vancouver

Small Business Series:

The Untaught Curriculum

Bootstrapped and Thriving

The Everyday Entrepreneur's Playbook

Reject and Build

Don't miss out!

Visit the website below and you can sign up to receive emails whenever Ryan Thompson publishes a new book. There's no charge and no obligation.

https://books2read.com/r/B-A-YDUUC-BNSIF

Connecting independent readers to independent writers.

Did you love *Beyond the Treeline*? Then you should read *Packwood*[1] by Ryan Thompson!

[2]

Trapped in a concrete cell with no memory of how she got there, Margaret Swanson wakes to a nightmare she can't explain. A pounding headache and a name stitched onto a gray jumpsuit are all she has left of her identity. When a stern man introduces himself as Keith Peterson, the Secretary of Homeland Security, he brings troubling revelations. Margaret isn't just a victim of her circumstances; she's the key to stopping Dr. Seth Myelin, a rogue mastermind tied to the infamous MKUltra program. Haunting shadows of her erased past may hold the secret to thwarting an impending disaster.

Set in the misty reaches of a Pacific Northwest town, *Packwood* is a high stakes blend of mystery and suspense. Margaret must grapple with

---

1. https://books2read.com/u/4jJMNZ

2. https://books2read.com/u/4jJMNZ

questions of trust and self worth while piecing together who she really is. Her mission is daunting, but her drive for redemption burns brighter than her fears.

This gripping thriller dives deep into resilience, buried secrets, and the aching hope of second chances. With vivid characters and a twist filled narrative, *Packwood* will keep you on the edge of your seat. Will Margaret find the courage to confront her past before time runs out? Read the first installment of the Margaret Swanson Series and discover her unforgettable journey.

Read more at https://eppublishers.com.

About the Author

Ryan Thompson is a passionate entrepreneur and author with a diverse background in the hospitality, technology, and non-profit sectors. Drawing from years of experience founding and managing businesses, Ryan brings a unique perspective to his work. His debut book, *Beyond The Treeline*, was published in 2024, inspired by the legacy of his late father, whose love for exploring influenced Ryan's own creative pursuits. He currently has many books published under his name with many more in development. He lives in Idaho with his wife, finding joy and inspiration in the life they share together.

Read more at https://eppublishers.com.